Jesus
Our Perfect Example

"I have set you an example that you should do as I have done for you." John 13:15

Written by Lori Merrill

Jesus, Our Perfect Example

ISBN-13: 978-1-935651-20-8

Edited by Brett Currie, Renee Corley and Diane Gardner
Cover design by Eric Granata
Interior design by Debbie Hammett
Cover Image by Felix Möckel

Printed in the United States of America

15 14 13 12 11   1 2 3 4 5 6 7 8

For additional resources, or to contact Lori Merrill, go to www.keepersministry.com

I dedicate this book to my husband Steve
who has, in so many ways, been a reminder
of God's grace in my life.

Contents

How It Began

God began to work in my heart about writing in May 2000. It had never occurred to me before that I would write a study someday. I knew I would teach, but never had I thought about writing. I kept feeling a nudge from the Lord that I needed to write, and as the nudge became a push, I began asking questions of Him: "Lord, *what* would I write?"and, "*Why* would you want me to write?" Then of course, the very practical, "But I don't know *how* to write!" I promised Him that I would continue to seek Him in this area, and as I went on with my teaching, I kept feeling Him push me harder and harder to write. I kept reminding Him that I didn't know how to write!

Then He did it. You know what I'm talking about—His precious, sweet way of making me feel silly and almost foolish. As I was having lunch with a group of women from the Bible study I was teaching, one of them asked the question, "So, do you write all of the material that you teach each week?" It was as if God Himself asked me the question. I paused and realized, indeed I did. I answered with a grin, "Yes, I do." God reminded me through this realization that I had been right—*I* could not write, just like every week *I* could not teach. He would do it through me. He was teaching me each week what He wanted me to learn so that I in turn could teach others about Him. This took sacrifice and discipline—the discipline to choose to spend time with Him in prayer and in His Word, so that I could hear clearly from Him about what to teach and write in my lesson every week. At that moment, I giggled within myself and thanked Him. He did indeed want me to write.

Something amazing happened that day. I surrendered to His will for me to write. Now I needed to know *what* to write. I began to pray and ask Him. Every week as I studied and every week as I taught, one phrase was a continual refrain, "Jesus is our perfect example." This was what I kept hearing from God and what I kept repeating to the women in my study. No matter where in His Word I looked, this is what He showed me. Then it dawned on me (did I mention that I am slow sometimes?) that God wanted me to write about His Son.

He is what this study is about, and it is about living. It is about living a life of peace, contentment, and joy. How? We follow "Jesus, our Perfect Example."

"For I gave you an example that you also should do as I did to you."
John 13:15

My Thanks:

First and foremost to my heavenly Father who called and entrusted me to this task. I consider it nothing but an honor to serve You in this small way. Thank You for allowing me this privilege to share of Your love, goodness, and unending mercy in this manner! I am and will always remain eternally grateful for the gift of Your Son, Jesus.

To my husband Steve: For your constant support, encouragement, sacrifice, love, and (as always) your prayers. You see what I cannot. I am honored and blessed to be your wife.

Josh, Jonathan, and Brooke: For your love, patience, sacrifice, and support. Your questions and heartfelt prayers are more encouraging than I could ever express. May you seek His example always. I am honored and blessed to be your mom!

My faithful prayer partners: You have persevered in prayer for me before and throughout this process. You will never know what a difference your prayers made until you meet Him in heaven, but I can tell you that I felt prayed for and encouraged by each of you every step of the way. Thank you, dear friends!

Brett: For your dedication and commitment to editing this assignment from the moment I asked. God provided you at just the right time in my life (no surprise). You were always encouraging no matter how late it became! Thanks for your precious prayers as well. I value your friendship.

Dennis and Marcia: Marcia, you have always been that sweet friend who encourages me to step out in faith. You somehow see more in me than I can see. God used you to confirm that this was indeed the time. Dennis, thanks for being a faithful pastor who teaches truth and for always being willing to answer my questions.

Renee and Debbs: Thanks for your willingness to come along in the final stages and use your talents to do what was necessary to bring it together. You are a reminder of God's faithfulness to complete His task in His time.

In His Love,

Lori

Introduction

There are just a few things you need to know before you begin this study. This study consists of eight lessons. It is divided into weekly lessons consisting of five days for each lesson topic. Each lesson will begin with a verse to memorize and a prayer. Please take both of these very seriously. The verse I have chosen will coincide with the lesson for the week. I ask that you meditate on this verse each day and do your best to memorize it. I suggest that you copy the memory verse onto an index card and carry it with you during the week or use it as a bookmark for your Bible or notebook. To hide God's Word in our hearts is so very important to our spiritual growth.

The prayer that you will read is my prayer to the Father that I have prayed on behalf of anyone who would do this study. Each prayer includes the goals that I believe the Lord has led me to accomplish for that particular lesson. Please join me in praying the same on your behalf.

The most important thing you will ever do before you begin each lesson is to take a few moments to pray for the Lord to teach you and speak to you through His Word. I am not the one who will make the difference in your life, nor will my writing. Rather it is the Holy Spirit who will prompt you and teach you "great and mighty things which you do not know," if you will ask this of Him (see Jeremiah 33:3). So, I strongly encourage you to pause and pray before each and every lesson.

Finally, as I write about Christ, please never forget that I adore Him, and my intentions would never be to diminish who He is. While I may compare our actions, our responses, and how we should live each day to Him, I am not in any way implying that you or I could ever be on the same level. I know He is God, but I also know that He was somehow God and man in the flesh. I don't understand it fully, but I believe it with all my heart. I have gained so much hope from His example because I realize that He was faced with the same temptations which I have been faced with. It also gives me so much comfort to know that I can overcome any temptation because the Holy Spirit lives within me to conform me to the image of God's Son, Jesus! Thank you for taking this magnified look at the example of our Lord Jesus Christ with me. May we both never be the same again!

A word about the cover . . .

The cover idea is an answered prayer. While praying for a cover that would reflect the message that God wanted conveyed, the Lord prompted me to ask my son Jonathan to draw something for me. I gave him ideas and asked him to pray about it. At the time he was twelve years old. You can see his original design on the next page, just the way it appeared on our first homework packet. I hope you see the message in the design. We want to be Jesus Christ's shadow, His reflection. Our desire should be to follow Him so intently that when people see us, they see Him. They see us following His example so closely that we are but a mere shadow of the cross, thereby giving glory and honor to Him!

Week 1

Jesus: His Example of Prayer

"But Jesus Himself would often slip away to the wilderness and pray." Luke 5:16

Day 1
Jesus Taught Us to Abide

Day 2
Are You Abiding?

Day 3
Jesus Made Time to Pray

Day 4
Jesus Was Dependent on Prayer

Day 5
Jesus Taught Us How to Pray

Memory and Meditation Verse: "Then you will call upon Me and come and pray to Me, and I will listen to you." Jeremiah 29:12

Prayer: *Our precious heavenly Father, Lord, I beseech You on behalf of every person who would do this study to see through the Word and words to You. Teach us to see so much more than parables or stories and see how Jesus lived so that we would know how to live. Lord, this week I pray that we will see how prayer was so important to Christ, how He lived a life of seeking You and depending on You no matter what He faced. Lord, may You transform us through our study this week to become passionate, persistent, and fervent in our prayers. Help us to see how our prayer life is a vital part of a firm foundational relationship with You. Bless this week of study and the efforts put forth, dear Father.* **Amen.**

Week 1

Jesus: His Example of Prayer

"But Jesus Himself would often slip away to the wilderness and pray." Luke 5:16

Welcome! I am so excited that God has called you to this study and that you and I together can intently seek Christ's example for living. The most difficult part of writing has been getting started. Not because starting is that difficult in and of itself, but because the desire to begin in the right place is so very important. I know what God wants me to accomplish by writing this study; I know what God has laid on my heart to write about. However, I cannot ensure that each person is at the same place in their life to receive this book. That is something only God can do. I do not know who will eventually read this study and who will actually do the study, so it has been hard for me to determine a "starting place" for us. Therefore, I believe it is very important to establish some common ground.

God sent His one and only Son to die for us so that we might live eternally with Him. Jesus went to the cross for you. He went to the cross for me. God loves us so much that He sacrificed His Son so that we, who needed a Savior, would have one.

Jesus Christ. I love Him with all my heart, soul, mind, and strength and hope to love Him even more with each day, month, and year that passes. I hope that is your testimony as well. Jesus is my Savior, and He can be your Savior too! God sent His one and only Son to die for us so that we might live eternally with Him. Jesus went to the cross for you. He went to the cross for me. God loves us so much that He sacrificed His Son so that we, who needed a Savior, would have one. He is the only way to heaven. He is the only way to the Father. In John 14:6, Jesus said, "I am the way, and the truth, and the life; no one comes to the Father but through Me." God says in His Word that "all have sinned and fall short of the glory of God" (Romans 3:23). God's Word also states in John 3:16-17 that "God so loved the world, that He gave His only begotten Son, that whoever believes in Him shall not perish, but have eternal life. For God did not send the Son into the world to judge the world, but that the world might be saved through Him." Jesus. You cannot separate Him from the one true, living God. He was sent to earth because you and I needed a Savior from our sins. I believe He was also sent so that you and I could see how to live. He died on the cross for our sins so we could be saved. And then He rose on the third day so we could live eternally. Believe in your heart and confess with your mouth that He is the Son of God and the Savior for your sins, and you will live eternally with Him. Jesus. Let Him be our common ground.

DAY 1: *Jesus Taught Us to Abide*

I need you to realize that this week's subject is the foundation of the entire study. Everything else will be built upon this foundation, so please don't miss one part of it. If we don't come to an understanding here in this first week, then the rest of the study will be more difficult for you. Why do I say that? Because every subject I write about—how to confront someone, how to love someone, how to forgive like Christ Jesus—will take prayer, and oodles of it. I could not have learned what I have about living a life pleasing to the Father without prayer. Through prayer I have been changed. Through prayer I have loved, I have forgiven, and I have had the courage to confront—all as Jesus did. You can too! All the subjects in this study will require prayer. So, don't start this week—or one day—without asking in prayer for our precious heavenly Father to do a mighty work in your life.

As I begin to write about the subject of prayer, so much floods my mind that I am not sure where and how to begin. I have a deep-seated passion for prayer. If you were to ask me why, I don't know if I could tell you all the reasons except to say that I *know* that I know it works. I have witnessed the miracles of prayer—I am one of them. My husband is as well. We have three wonderful children who would qualify as "answers" to prayer. Some have told me I have a gift for prayer; others have said I have the gift of intercession. I am not sure if I agree; all I know is that I have found—tried and true—that God does answer prayer! Prayer does change things. I believe the more I see the power of prayer, the more I believe and can't help but pray. You see, I have traveled through the dark days. I have been where I feel as if there is no tomorrow, and I have realized that all people will disappoint and hurt me—no matter how much they love me. There is only One who will never leave me nor forsake me (see Hebrews 13:5), and it is to Him I turn in prayer.

What is prayer? Prayer is communication with God, conversation with God. We will look more at this communication with the Father after we establish how important it is. Let's start by looking at a familiar passage in the New Testament, John 15. Precious and wonderful words are spoken here by Jesus. Let these words soak into your mind, and contemplate what God wants you to see and learn.

Before you begin reading, first understand a few things. Jesus is the one speaking here, so in verse 1 when He says, "I am the true vine," He is talking about Himself. Then He goes on to say, "My Father is the vinedresser." As we read on, we learn that we (those who know Jesus and have a personal relationship with Him) are the branches. Taking the following into consideration, read John 15:1-11.

True vine—Jesus
Vinedresser—God the Father
Branches—Christians

Now answer the following questions:

What happens to the branches that do not bear fruit? (vs. 2)______________________

____

____

What happens to the branches that bear fruit? (vs. 2) Why?______________________

____

____

Reread verses 4 and 5. Can the branch bear fruit without the vine? ______________

____

What must the branch do to bear fruit?____

____

____

How many times is the word *abide* (NIV states "remain") used in this passage?

Because this word is repeated over and over again, it is a key word, and God wanted us to learn something very important about this word. The word translated "abide" is the Greek word *meno*.[1] It means "to stay, abide, remain, to dwell." In reference to a state or condition, it means "to remain as one, not to become another or different."

Do you think Jesus fully understood His ministry and His purpose on this earth?

Could He do all that He did and do it successfully without the Father?

Jesus knew the mission for which He was sent and knew how vital it was to abide with the Father. Let's ask ourselves this question: If Jesus needed to abide with the Father, how much more should I?

According to verse 5, what can we do apart from Jesus Christ?

The word translated "nothing" in verse 5 means the absolute negative. In other words, He is not saying that you can do some things or partial things, but rather no things. So it really means just that—nothing. There is nothing that we can do apart from Him—Jesus Christ.

This should be inspiration enough for us to make some changes as needed in each of our lives. Knowing that we can do nothing apart from Him should push us to be with Him more, to seek to truly abide in Him. How do we do that? Let me share an illustration with you.

I am a very practical and visual person, so sometimes I need things to be made very simple for me to fully grasp the meaning. For example, I love it when someone gives me something to do and then gives me step-by-step instructions. In this instance, I can relate our choices about abiding to trying to assemble toys. I'll never forget one Christmas when Steve and I bought my daughter a three-story dollhouse that was mine to assemble. And I do mean truly assemble—right down to flowers in the flowerpots outside the house and the front-porch stairs. Sound detailed? It was! I took one look at it and was overwhelmed, but then I opened up the huge, multi-folded instruction sheet to see instructions and step-by-step pictures to go along with it. It did take me half the day (literally), but I wasn't overwhelmed. In fact, I enjoyed it.

This holds true for our walk with the Lord. There are a myriad of disciplines we could practice to become more Christlike, things that would help us "look" more like Him. However, without intimacy with Him, these disciplines profit nothing. They are just that, disciplines. Yes, we may become more self-disciplined because of them, but God's Word states that discipline done for such reasons profits us little. Godliness is profitable for all things (see 1 Timothy 4:8). So, we need to *first* do the things which are of primary importance to our growth and spiritual well-being. Reading God's Word and spending time with Him in prayer are two primary ways to abide. These two should be a priority in our lives. Just as we shouldn't continue to build a house without the firm foundation established, so it is in our relationship with the Lord.

I always think of it this way: "If Jesus did this or that, then how much more should I?" Jesus is a part of the Trinity. He was God and man—tempted like us with the ability to sin, yet He didn't. He was and is perfect. So, when we look at all the examples of Christ through this study, always think of it in this way: Jesus prayed (loved, obeyed . . .) how much more should I?

Jesus knew how important it was to abide. One reason He lived such a successful life—could face temptation and not sin, could be abused and not hurl insults, could love when there was nothing to love about someone or love the very ones who hurt Him—is because He abided with His Father. You and I are called to do the same! We are told over and over again in these eleven verses to abide in Him. If He is our priority, we will be abiding with Him and in Him. We will be dwelling in Him, in His Word, and in fellowship with Him. We will allow our days to revolve around what is important to Him, and not what is important to us or to this world we live in.

Now let me ask some very personal questions.

Is daily intake of God's Word and prayer with Him a priority in your life? In other words, do you abide in Jesus?

Do you make every effort to be with Him every day?

If you answered no to either of these questions, then what keeps you from abiding?

If He is not your priority, then I would say, based on Scripture, that you are not bearing the fruit that God planned for you to bear (see John 15:4). Let's face it, we all make time to do the things that we really want to do or think are important to do. We also have things that happen that keep us from our time alone with Him every now and then. But I do hope and pray that these times become more infrequent!

Jesus knew how very important it was to make time to pray. In His daily life, He lived in a spirit of prayer. He abided with the Father. Therefore He knew who to teach, where to go, and whom to heal. Think about it. God's Word never states that Jesus healed *everyone*. In fact, it says in Mark 1:34 and 3:10 that he healed *many* who came to Him.

Jesus knew the importance of prayer and exemplified it. He was led by the Father in every aspect of His life and walk. It is Him who we are to imitate and it is His example that we are to follow. Will you?

Write your prayer to Him right now, dedicating yourself to making Him your number-one priority in life. He is worth it!____

____

____

____

We covered a lot of ground today. We began laying that firm foundation so necessary to this study and our lives. Tomorrow we will look at our own foundation and see how firm it really is.

DAY 2: *Are You Abiding?*

I made it clear in every way when introducing this study that this would be introspective. How can it not be? It is grounded in God's Word, which is truth because He is Truth. If you are in this study just to gain more intellectual knowledge about Jesus or God's Word, then you have the wrong attitude. Hopefully you *will* gain a lot more knowledge along the way. However, for me, the most important and exciting part of studying God's Word is the personal application. I ask you to stop right now and spend a couple of minutes asking Him to make clear what He wants you to learn today about yourself and about your life. May the Lord bless your obedience to dig into His Word.

Read Matthew 15:29-39.

This is one of the stories of Jesus feeding the thousands with seven loaves of bread and a few small fish and having food left over. (This is a different miracle from the one performed with the boy and five loaves and two fish found in John 6:5-15) Many of us know, especially if we have fasted, what it feels like to go without food for a day or more. These people were hungry! Reread verse 32.

How long had they been with Jesus?

I loved it when Jesus said to His disciples, "I feel compassion for the people." It is so God and yet so human. Why did Jesus say that He felt compassion for the people? "They have ______________________ with Me now three days and have nothing to eat."

This Scripture was so convicting to me some years ago when I read it. Three days. These people wanted to be with Jesus so much that they followed Him three days, with little concern for their sustenance. Since most people joined Jesus as they saw Him along the way, then I would assume that these people faced quite a journey home, hungry, and with little provision.

That is why Jesus was concerned about them fainting along the way. They couldn't drive through or walk to the nearest fast-food restaurant like we can. Nor did they have the modern conveniences which we are accustomed to, such as prepackaged food or local food marts. Consider this: Most of us are used to a steady intake of food, so if we miss one day it is a shock to our system, we become faint, and (if you are like me) think you are going to die! These people were consumed with Christ and following Him. They wanted to see Him, to be with Him, to be close to Him. They wanted it so badly that they didn't care if they didn't get to eat. They were so hungry *for* Him that they were willing to feel hunger *because* of Him. Another interesting point is that many of these

These people were consumed with Christ and following Him. They wanted to see Him, to be with Him, to be close to Him. They wanted it so badly that they didn't care if they didn't get to eat. They were so hungry* for *Him that they were willing to feel hunger* because *of Him.

people were probably small-business owners or farmers. A day away from work meant a day without pay. This would have impacted their ability to meet their personal needs beyond just that day's food.

For just a moment, let's imagine the scene. It reminds me of a rock concert. There were 4,000 men, plus women and children, and probably everyone wanted to get front-row seats! When I see pictures of concerts and people throwing themselves toward the rock stars and reaching out just to be touched, I cannot help but think that some of Jesus' experiences must have been this way. Except for one very different quality—peacefulness. I also cannot help but think about the way people respond to someone famous. Girls go crazy and become faint if they even get close to or touch their modern-day idol. We cannot even fathom what will happen some day when the only One who deserves to be worshiped returns. God tells us in His Word that one day *every* knee will bow and *every* tongue will confess that Jesus Christ is Lord (see Philippians 2:10-11). They won't have any control over themselves—even if they never, ever knew Him before, they will bow, and they will confess! They will have to, because it is truth; He is Truth! It gives me chills just thinking about it. Now, allow yourself to picture the scene and what it must have been like for Jesus to have 4,000 men, plus women and children, following Him for three days and then to have to feed them. Those poor disciples—I would give anything to get a glimpse of their faces when Jesus said He was going to feed them. This proclamation would make even Martha Stewart shudder!

Now I want you to see something else. Look with me again at Matthew 15:32. Jesus said, "I feel compassion for the people, because they have *remained* with Me now three days and have nothing to eat; and I do not want to send them away hungry, for they might faint on the way" (emphasis mine).

Remember the word *abide* that we looked at yesterday in John 15:1-10? We learned that it is the Greek word *meno*[2] and it means, "to remain as one, not to become another or different" It is a derivative of the word *prosmeno*,[3] which means "to remain with, continue with one." This word translated "remained" in verse 32 is *prosmeno*. Do you see what I see? These people were abiding! They were remaining with Jesus, abiding with Jesus for three days! He was their priority. He was who they desired to be with above all else—even food.

While being under the conviction of the Holy Spirit when I read this a few years ago, I wondered aloud what I would do to follow Jesus. What would I give up? How far would I go? We all know what we want to answer, what we should answer. Would you follow Jesus three days without food just to be near Him? If you and I are honest, our lives right now answer for us. No matter what we write for the answer, no matter what we say we will do or intend to do, there is no denying—the answer is spoken to God and Jesus Himself every day through the choices we make.

Has He called you to give up something to follow Him?

If so, what is it, and will you do it?

In His Word, Jesus says,

"If anyone wishes to come after Me, he must deny himself, and take up his

cross daily and follow Me." (Luke 9:23)

and

"For where your treasure is, there your heart will be also." (Matthew 6:21)

If He has spoken to you as He has to me through this, will you write your prayer to Him now? It is so important to be cleansed of the past, even if that means yesterday, this morning, or just hours ago. If the Lord wants you to make changes, listen and write them now. If you have neglected making Him a priority in your life, then all you have to do is tell Him about it and confess to Him that you have been wrong. ____

____

____

____

Now go one step further, and ask Him to enable you to make Him first every day. I believe it is so important to write spiritual events like this down on paper. So, I ask you to do it now and date it so some day you can come back and read it. May the Lord bless this sweet time between you and Him.

DAY 3: *Jesus Made Time to Pray*

There is no denying that prayer was an important part of Jesus' earthly life. And there is no doubt that Jesus made the time to pray. Just as I stated yesterday, we make time to do the things that are a priority to us. No matter what kind of a job we have, how old we are, how many children we have, or what ministry we serve in, we all have one thing in common: We each are given the same amount of time each day. We cannot look at someone else's life and think, "Well, I would serve the Lord in this way if I had their life." There is no excuse, because no matter what we say or what we do, it comes back to the choices we make.

Jesus made the choice to pray.

Read Mark 1:28-37, then focus on verses 32-35.

In my mind I am feeling the pressure! The previous day Jesus had a full schedule of appointments. Everyone wanted to be seen by the Great Physician. Can you imagine what His appointment book looked like? And you thought your wait at the doctor's office was bad! Now the sun had set and He was probably settling in for a nice, quiet rest, only to find every ill or demon-possessed person, not to mention the entire city, waiting for Him—at His door!

Now after an evening full of healing more and more people, along with casting out demons, Jesus rose early in the morning to do what?

Why do you think Jesus went to pray?

Why do you pray?

Do you only go to God in prayer when there is a crisis in your life?

Is He your first resort or your last?

When something upsets you in the normal course of your day, do you run to the phone or His throne?

I think it is normal for us to run to our spouse, a trusted friend, or a confidante when things happen that upset us. But do you realize that God promises to be all those for us, and He is better than any earthly relationship we could ever have? I am not suggesting that you don't talk to these people in your life when you are troubled. However, where do you run first?

Read Psalm 9:10. Write what this verse means to you.

If you know Him, you will trust Him. In fact, the more you know Him, the more you trust Him. He never forsakes those who seek Him. What a wonderful promise from the Lord. I have to tell you that I had to hold tight to this promise and many others while writing this study. When God called me to write it, He had been working in my life to prepare me. I had never previously written a study from scratch. The work reflects nothing of me; rather it came out of simple obedience and love for Him. While in the throes of doing what He had called me to do, I found the process painfully slow and very laborious at times. I struggled to hear what He wanted me to write. I wrote and rewrote more than I could count. I became scared at times, anxious, and very frustrated. But each and every time temptation came, I had to give it to God. Not only did I give it to Him, but I prayed to Him. I talked out loud and silently about Philippians 4:6-7 at least once every hour those days. "Be anxious for nothing (Lori), but in everything (Lori) by prayer and supplication with thanksgiving let your (Lori's) requests be made known to God. And the peace of God, which surpasses all comprehension, will guard your (Lori's) hearts and your minds in Christ Jesus." I had to remind myself of His promises.

While the writing may not have happened on my time schedule and according to my deadlines, it happened. And though we live in a day and time where there is so much uncertainty about the future, this I know for sure—God can never go against His character or His Word. His Word states that His character does not forsake those who seek Him. So, as I recalled His promises and reminded myself of His Word and His character, I became peaceful. It doesn't mean that words flowed more easily at that moment. It does mean, however, that God supplied all I needed in His time because I sought Him and obeyed Him.

I am sure Jesus could have come up with a million reasons to not get up early to go out and pray. The primary reason for me would be sleep—can you relate? Make a commitment to Him right now to choose prayer. Choose it over sleep, a full schedule, fear, and frustration. Write your desire below to choose praying to Him over all other things.

Dear heavenly Father, may You bless our desire and our efforts to make the time to pray and to choose to pray over all else.

DAY 4: *Jesus Was Dependent on Prayer*

Jesus knew what kingdom work needed to be done each and every day. Therefore, He needed to fellowship with the Father, depend on the Father, and draw His strength from the Father. Look up the following verses noting what Jesus did and who He was with.

Matthew 14:23

Matthew 26:39

Mark 1:35

Mark 6:46

Luke 6:12

Luke 22:44

Obviously Jesus modeled prayer for Matthew, Mark, and Luke as well as the rest of us. Here, by their accounts, we see many times that Jesus made prayer a priority. I think these verses give you some idea of how important prayer was to Jesus.

Now look up Luke 3:21 and answer the following questions.

What was happening to Jesus at this time?

While He was being baptized what was He doing?

Now read Luke 6:6-13. Jesus had just healed a man's withered hand on the Sabbath, which did not make the Pharisees happy campers! In fact, it filled them with so much anger and rage that they had a little meeting to see what they might do to Jesus. It would make me want to laugh if I didn't feel such compassion for their blindness as to who He was. Think of the irony in the statement, "And discussed together what they might do to Jesus." If they only would have known that they couldn't have lifted one finger against Him without the Father allowing them.

As the scribes and Pharisees discussed what they might do to Him, where and what did Jesus go to do?

Let's reflect on what Jesus did and what we can learn from His example. Jesus was faced with the Pharisees and their rage. He was misunderstood constantly. Please don't let yourself forget that though He was God, He was God in the flesh. He was there to die for the Pharisees just as much as He died for you and me. He was their Savior, and they misunderstood His purpose behind each act. How it must have hurt Him. If you are like me, you know what it is like to be misunderstood. For people to think the worst of us instead of the best is painful. Write about a time you have been misunderstood.____

____

____

____

____

Now be like Christ and take it to the Lord in prayer. Tell Him of your pain and how it made you feel. He understands because He was misunderstood and knows every hurt and every bit of pain you feel.

How long did Jesus pray?

And when day came, what did Jesus do?

What do you think Jesus prayed about?

Though Scripture does not always tell us what Jesus prayed about, we can make some assumptions based on the circumstances surrounding His prayers. We see here that Jesus chose His twelve apostles after spending all night in prayer. Jesus teaches us here that He prayed about and through everything. This is 1 Thessalonians 5:17 in action. My husband and I refer to what we have learned from these verses in this way: To pray without ceasing is to remain in a "spirit of prayer." I don't know how else to describe it. Some years ago when I asked God how to pray without ceasing, He reminded me of the following: Many times in my day things do not go as planned—I know that you can relate. How do you handle daily events such as difficulties with children, a hurtful word said by a loved one (or a stranger), or an unexpected event? Well, I can tell you that I usually don't handle them well unless I am in a spirit of prayer—talking to God all day long. "How do I handle this one, Lord?" "What do I do now, Lord?" "Help me hold my tongue, Lord!" You get the idea. If it were left up to me and my fleshly response, I would dishonor the Word of God (see Titus 2:5) and not be a good testimony. Being in a spirit of prayer isn't just about the negative things that come up, but about the positive as well (like Jesus talking to His Father while being baptized). I really talk to Him all day long; He is my Friend, my Father, my Confidante, and my Everything!

Do you talk to Him all day long?

Why? What is He to you?

Praise Him for it!

I talk to Him about the good things that are happening, about choices I need to make, I pray for someone as He puts them on my mind, and the list goes on and on. Don't think that you have to be on your knees beside your bed with your eyes closed to pray to our Lord. That is a great place to be, but how many of us can spend our days there?

To wrap up our lesson for today, let's just review some of the great examples of Jesus and His prayer life:

1. Jesus abided with the Father through prayer.
2. Jesus prayed alone and with others.
3. Jesus prayed when making decisions.
4. Jesus prayed during joyous times and difficult times.
5. Jesus prayed all night when needed.

Lord, I pray for us to be willing to put aside whatever presses in on us so we can come to Your throne and sit at Your feet in prayer. Amen.

DAY 5: *Jesus Taught Us How to Pray*

Yesterday we learned about Jesus modeling prayer for us. What an awesome mentor He is! I love that God has placed earthly mentors in my life. Sometimes these are women I watch from afar. At times they have been women I work alongside in a particular ministry. Other times they have been women God wants me to interview and ask some questions for just a few minutes, whether by phone or in person. There are people all around us whom we can learn from. I tell women all the time, "Someone is always watching you." You are a testimony, whether positive or negative, to someone even when you aren't aware of it. I am a watcher. I look for God in everything. I have learned more from watching how others do something than I ever have from talking to them about how they do something. I discover positive and negative examples—the way I believe God would want me to do it and the way God would not want me to do something. God wants me to learn from other people as long as I don't place them before Him by making them an idol. It can be easy to idolize a person when we see someone truly godly we want to emulate. We need to be careful and remember that what we are seeing is the Holy Spirit within them and working through them. Yes, we can learn so much from others, and it is okay to admire and respect their walk with the Lord. However, we need to remember that there is no one person who has her life all together, wrapped in a perfect package. Only Jesus lived up to that. The great thing about Jesus is that He didn't stop with just modeling prayer for us. When asked by His disciples, He also told us how to do it.

I know prayer can be intimidating to so many. It once was to me as well. I think the more we realize that there isn't a magic formula for prayer, the better we feel about it. God did give us an example for prayer, however. Can you imagine what we might have done to prayer if He hadn't? There is no telling what kind of crazy requirements and formulas we might have tried to create. We are just that way as humans, aren't we? I know we must make God laugh at times because we have such legalistic tendencies. We want to have boxes for everything to fit into. But remember, prayer is still nothing more than communication with our heavenly Father. It is a conversation with God, and when you think of it in this way, it isn't so intimidating.

Read Matthew 6:5-13, then look at verses 5 and 6 to see what Jesus was teaching:

> ***"When you pray, you are not to be like the hypocrites; for they love to stand and pray in the synagogues and on the street corners so that they may be seen by men. Truly I say to you, they have their reward in full. But you, when you pray, go into your inner room, close your door and pray to your Father who is in secret, and your Father who sees what is done in secret will reward you."***

I believe we can learn several things from these two verses.

1. **Do not use prayer to prove your righteousness.**
   Jesus was saying that these hypocrites love to stand in the synagogues and on the street corners to by seen by others. The word *hypocrite* means "an actor, a pretender." The word for *seen* means "to bring forth into the light, cause to shine." Obviously by these meanings there were people who prayed as an "act" so that people could see them and deem them righteous. I love how God's Word can come alive right before our eyes, don't you? Think about an actor and his job. What actor wants to be hidden? The very nature of his job is to be seen, to be in the spotlight. How many actors do you know who want to be an extra in a movie or a play rather than wanting to be the star? Maybe at first an aspiring actor is happy with any role, but soon their expectations grow and their goal is to be seen! The hypocrites Jesus mentioned were pretending, or acting righteous so that others would notice them, and they loved the attention!

Based on this information, how many of their prayers do you think were sincere?

Read 1 Samuel 16:7 and note what man sees compared to what the Lord sees.

Man:

The Lord:

So, what did Jesus see when He looked at the hypocrites?

This reminds me of the famous quote by Abraham Lincoln, "You can fool all the people some of the time, and some of the people all the time, but you cannot fool all the people all of the time." And you can never fool God. He knows our hearts even better than we do!

2. **Prayer alone with the Father is vital to your abiding.**
   Jesus was not saying that you should not pray with others. We see in Scripture where Jesus prayed with others; He prayed in front of others as well as prayed while others were with Him. We can see in Scripture many examples of believers praying together, and the importance of praying with others is stressed in Matthew 18:20, "For where two or three have gathered together in My name, I am there in their midst." However, the majority of the time, when we look at the examples of Jesus praying, He was alone. I believe that Matthew 6:5-6 warns against becoming like the hypocrites. I also believe that regular prayer time alone with our Father is vital to a growing and vibrant relationship with our Lord. We must be careful to not allow our times of

prayer with others to substitute for our time of prayer alone. I have learned firsthand that when my *personal* prayer life slips, even though I am deeply studying God's Word and in prayer with others, my walk with the Father is weakened. (Refer back to John 15:4-5, which we studied this week.) A steady, regular, daily intake of God's Word and time in prayer with Him is vital to abiding.

3. **God rewards a life of prayer.**
   Rewards come in many ways, but the biggest blessing for me that has come from my prayer life is my deepened relationship with Him. I trust Him more because I pray, and I have seen His faithfulness no matter what situation I face. My faith in Him has grown because I have seen Him answer prayers. My faith also has grown because I have seen Him *not* answer my prayers, only to later see that His will for me was better than I could have imagined. Then there are the still unanswered prayers. Yet even through these, my faith, hope, and trust are strengthened as I learn over and over again that His plan is always better than anything I could have conceived. Rewards can come in many forms and be many things—peace, contentment, material rewards, etc.—but nothing can compare to the reward of knowing Him better!

Jesus continued His teaching in Matthew 6:7-8.

"And when you are praying, do not use meaningless repetition as the Gentiles do, for they suppose that they will be heard for their many words. So do not be like them; for your Father knows what you need before you ask Him."

Jesus wanted to teach us what not to do so that we would know better what to do. The Gentiles were pagans. They were people "alien to the worship of the true God."[4] The word *suppose* means "an opinion." Their opinion was that if they used many words over and over again, they would be heard. How important it is that we don't base our knowledge of God and His character on our own opinions. We will fail every time. When we don't understand why He is who He says He is and why He does what He does, we need to accept it. We cannot only accept that which we understand. God tells us in Isaiah 55:8-9,

***"For My thoughts are not your thoughts,
Nor are your ways
My ways," declares the Lord.
"For as the heavens are
higher than the earth,
so are My ways higher than your ways
and My thoughts than your thoughts."***

Do you have "opinions" of God and His character that have led to disappointment or anger with God?

If so, what are they?

Understanding and accepting these verses requires faith in action. One of my children used to ask questions about God and His ability to be who He says He is. At times my son would ask so many questions that it would scare me. He had already invited Christ into his life years before, but his questions were questions of doubt to me. When he first began asking these questions, I would try to come up with answers to convince him. Of course, I wanted to convince him, but I think more than that I was scared I didn't really know the answers. I took these questions seriously. I began praying on his behalf against the attacks of the enemy. I didn't know if this was the enemy trying to make my son doubt his salvation and his God. But in case it was the enemy, I was not going to give in without a fight. I also realized this could have been his natural curiosity. So, as I prayed about it, this is what I told him based on Isaiah 55:8-9: "There will be things that you or I never understand about God. He tells us in His Word that His ways and thoughts are above our own. Just as salvation takes faith to believe in what we cannot see, so do all these unanswered questions. Son, you have to trust God. It is okay to ask these things of Him, but if you don't get the answers then you still must trust." Think about it; if we didn't have questions, then we wouldn't have faith.

Now move on in Matthew 6:7-8. Jesus tells us to not be like the Gentiles with their meaningless repetition because the Father knows what we need before we ask. I have heard people ask one of two things based on this verse. They have either wondered, "If the Father knows what I need before I ask, then why pray?" or "If I have asked once and He already knows, then why ask again?"

Verse 8 starts with, "So do not be like them." How would we be like them?

Talking to the Lord meaninglessly could be just as bad as not talking to Him at all. If you have no intention of truly speaking to Him, then they are mere words, like a script in a play. This is what the Gentiles were doing. They didn't know Him, so how could they have been speaking to Him? God does know what we need before we ask Him. If this surprises you, then you will be really surprised to hear that He also knows what you need before *you* know what you need! Why do we ask, then? Faith, discipline, diligence, perseverance, humility—just to name a few reasons. If anything, this should bring us relief. We don't have to start from scratch with every story to get every detail in. He already knows more details about the situation than you do. I am not suggesting that you cease pouring your heart out to God. I think He loves few things more than seeing and hearing His child tell the whole story. For us to feel that comfortable and to want to be with Him for that length of time is precious to Him.

Let's look at one more verse just so you can see that God does want you to go to Him in prayer. Look at Philippians 4:6-7 and fill in the blanks:

"Be anxious for nothing, but in ______________ by prayer and supplication with thanksgiving let your requests be _____________ ______________ to God."

Since we are to pray about everything and let every request be made known to God, I believe this is another charge for living in the "spirit of prayer."

According to verse 7, what happens if you do these things?

The ______________ of God . . . will _____________ your hearts and your minds in Christ Jesus.

Praise God that He wants to hear all things from us when we come to Him to truly speak to Him! I was cautioned about my prayers recently when I read the following statement written by Beth Moore. In talking about prayer, she wrote, "We save time when we don't tell God how to answer the prayer! God doesn't need our list of solutions." How true that is. We must be sure to remember He is our Father, but He is also Almighty God. We must approach His throne in reverent awe of who He is and praise Him that we have access to Him!

Now let's wrap up today by looking a little closer at the Lord's Prayer. Many years ago I learned about the Lord's Prayer from Kay Arthur's book *Lord, Teach Me to Pray in 28 Days* (© Kay Arthur, 2008: Harvest House Publishers, pp. 34-35: used by permission). I am grateful for the concepts about the Lord's Prayer that were ingrained in my mind from that study. I want to share with you the points that have helped me to understand this prayer. Breaking it into sections as Kay does in her study has proved beneficial to me.

Please remember that this is not a prayer that Jesus wanted us to simply recite when we pray to Him, though I don't believe that there is anything wrong with that. In Matthew 6:9 Jesus said, "Pray, then, in this way . . ." He did not say, "Pray this . . ." Jesus was giving us an example to follow.

Pray, then, in this way:
"Our Father who is in heaven,
Hallowed be Your name."

The first two lines of the Lord's Prayer teach us to address and approach the Lord with praise. We begin by praising Him and worshiping Him. When we praise Him for who He is, we cannot help but worship Him. This is a natural progression. Praise Him and tell Him who and what He is to you. Hallow His name, for it is holy.

"Your kingdom come.
Your will be done,
On earth as it is in heaven."

Here, we are to acknowledge Him and our allegiance to His kingdom and His sovereignty. In other words, His will first before our own. Pray whatever you must to align your will with His. We are to realize who He is and align ourselves in proper authority to Him.

Matthew 6:11 then asks:

"Give us this day our daily bread."

This is a representation of petition and intercession. We need to ask for His provision in our own lives and on behalf of others. Acknowledge Him as Jehovah-jireh, our Provider.

Matthew 6:12 requests God's forgiveness:

"And forgive us our debts, as we also have forgiven our debtors."

Here, we come to confession and forgiveness. At one time I was baffled that the example to ask for forgiveness was so far into the Lord's Prayer. Then I realized that at times it takes spending time with the Father before we recognize our sins. Of course, there are always times when we have heavy hearts because of sin in our lives and immediately we should and need to confess it. However, I find that most times the longer I am in His presence, because of His holiness, I am convicted. This seems to particularly happen while praising Him, celebrating His worth, and acknowledging His lordship. This is a natural response to examining ourselves in light of who He is.

And, finally, Matthew 6:13 closes the prayer:

"And do not lead us into temptation, but deliver us from evil. [For Yours is the kingdom and the power and the glory forever. Amen.]"[5]

In this verse we are being shown the importance of asking for protection, of remaining watchful, and of asking for guidance and deliverance. Then in closing, we are led once again to acknowledging who He is and worshiping Him. What about thanksgiving? Worship is adoration of Him. When we are praising Him and worshiping Him, we won't be able to help but thank Him. I believe thankfulness is a part of all the above. We are to do as Philippians 4:6 states, "in everything by prayer and supplication with thanksgiving let your requests be made known to God."

I give you all of this as a guide. The purpose is not to intimidate you more about prayer. I think you will find the next two verses of great comfort.

Let's first start with Romans 8:26.

Do we know how to pray as we should?

Who intercedes for us?

Now read verse 34. Based on this verse, where is Jesus?

What is He doing while there?

Wow! We not only have the Holy Spirit to help us to pray and to intercede for us, but we also have Jesus Christ, who is at the right hand of God interceding for us. Jesus, the one who faced all temptations that we could ever face and now intercedes for us at the right hand of the Father—don't you think He is the perfect one to intercede on our behalf? Do we have anything to worry about? No. Not when we go humbly before our God, with a heart for Him, seeking His face.

We began the first lesson of this week describing what prayer is. It is, simply stated, conversation with God. However, conversation does take two people, and proper conversation involves both parties conversing. Therefore, with all you have learned about Jesus and His example of prayer, don't forget one very important component: Jesus listened to His Father. He knew what to do, where to go, whom to heal, whom to choose, and more, because He listened. Make this part of your prayer life. Leave time during every conversation with the Father to sit and listen in silence. You will be amazed at what you hear the Father say. God bless you!

Week 2

Jesus: His Example of Obedience

"Being found in appearance as a man, He humbled Himself by becoming obedient to the point of death, even death on a cross." Philippians 2:8

Day 1
A Key Ingredient

Day 2
Obedience Requires Dependence and Humility

Day 3
Obedience Requires Sacrifice and Perseverance

Day 4
Obedience Requires Trust and Faith

Day 5
Do You Have Peace and Contentment?

Memory and Meditation Verse: "Blessed are those who hear the word of God and observe it." Luke 11:28

Prayer: *Lord, I praise Your holy name. I thank You for Your Son's example of obedience for us. Father, teach us this week how important obedience is to You and that it is a key ingredient to an abundant and effective life. Lord, I pray that we will realize the difference between partial and complete obedience as we examine our own lives in light of Your Word. And Lord, show us how to learn from the examples of Jesus in regard to His humility, His willingness to sacrifice, and His trust in Your plans above His own security and comfort. You are Adonai, our Lord and Master. May we have the desire and the courage to obey You above all else. In Jesus' name,* **Amen.**

Week 2

Jesus: His Example of Obedience

"Being found in appearance as a man, He humbled Himself by becoming obedient to the point of death, even death on a cross." Philippians 2:8

DAY 1: *A Key Ingredient*

Last week we looked at Jesus and the many examples of His prayer-filled life. We also had the opportunity to spend some time seeing how He taught us to pray and how He, along with the Holy Spirit, intercedes for us even now. This week we come to another subject that will continue to lay more foundation for a strong and productive spiritual life. Just as you cannot abide without an intake of God's Word and intimate prayer with Him, you cannot grow in your spiritual walk without obedience to Him. Prayer and obedience: These two subjects intertwine in many ways, and we find a natural progression from one to the other. If you have a prayerful life, then you will have many opportunities to be called to obedience. This obedience inspires many more prayers to help you carry out the call laid before you. You cannot be obedient without prayer, just as you cannot have intimate prayer without being called to obedience. A prayerful life leads to an obedient life. *An obedient life is a prayerful life*. That might sound redundant, but it isn't. Read it again and let it sink in.

From here throughout the rest of the study you will be faced with this subject of obedience. You will be making choices to obey or not to obey with every subject we study. Jesus lived a life of obedience. Scripture states that He was obedient to the point of death (see Philippians 2:8). To follow this example will take more than willpower. If obedience was just a matter of willpower, then many of us would have no problem with it. However, we all know that obeying God is much harder than that. Or maybe you think you are fine in this area and you have no problem obeying God. If this is the case, would you allow me to make a suggestion to you? Obedience to our Father is so much more than obeying the Ten Commandments or living a "good life." There is more to the Christian life and walk than that. Maybe that is the issue here. So many Christians think that this is all there is to being a Christian. I see so many who justify their Christianity this way. They are truly sincere about it. Please don't think I am being judgmental, but let me challenge your thinking just a bit. There are good people out there who do not know the Lord. What makes you different from them if you obey the Ten Commandments and nothing else? I believe that many live according to the Ten Commandments and because of this, they believe that they know and have a personal relationship with the Lord. If that was all there was to being a Christian, wouldn't you agree that the Christian life would be lacking? Oh, please don't make the mistake of believing this Christian life and walk is that simple and, may I say, that unfulfilling? On the other hand, there are others who believe (and sincerely, I might add) that the Christian life is drudgery. They believe it is boring, unexciting, and full of dos and don'ts. My husband laughs at how naïve he used to be as a young adult. He used to say, "The Christian life is so simple

Obedience to our Father is so much more than obeying the Ten Commandments or living a "good life."

if we will just do it." Many things have happened in his life and mine for us both to know that it isn't so simple to follow Christ. Yes, it is joyful, exhilarating, peaceful, wonderful, and more adjectives than I can name, but simple? No! If you find that you fall under either extreme, will you do me a favor? Will you ask the Lord right now to open your eyes and allow you to see beyond what you have been taught, what you have assumed, what you have allowed to become tradition to you? And for those of you who are somewhere in the middle, Stop and thank God, but also ask Him to continue to reveal to you anything that needs to change in your thinking and beliefs. Let's take a deeper look into this. Look up the following verses and fill in the blanks.

Acts 13:2—"While they were ministering to the Lord and fasting, the Holy Spirit said, '________________ ____________________ for Me Barnabas and Saul for the ______________________ ______________________ which I have called them.'"

Romans 1:1—"Paul, a bond-servant of Christ Jesus, ____________________ as an apostle, ____________________ ______________________ for the gospel of God."

Galatians 1:15-16—"But when God, who had ________________ ________________ ______________________ even from my mother's womb and ____________________ me through His grace, was pleased to reveal His Son in me so that I might preach Him among the Gentiles, I did not immediately consult with flesh and blood."

No doubt Saul, who was now Paul, knew what God called Him to do. He knew he had been "set apart." This word for "set apart" is the Greek word *aphorizo*.[6] It is the same word used in all three verses above, and it means "to appoint, to set apart for some purpose."

What had Paul been set apart for?

Did you know that you, too, have been set apart?

God does have a plan for you. I know that we look at Paul and we think that we could never ever accomplish what he did. But we can. It may not look exactly like Paul's ministry, but I guarantee you that it can be as effective. Let's look at a few verses together to see what God says about our own lives.

Read Psalm 139:13-16.

After reading these verses, are there any doubts in your mind that God planned for you to look the way you do, knew you before you were born, and ordained your days?

Do you think the same God who planned you and ordained your days has a plan for your life as well?

Read Jeremiah 29:11 and answer the following questions.

Who has plans for you?

What are His plans for you?

Now go on to verse 12.

What does God say He will do when we call upon and pray to Him?

In verse 13, what must we do to find the Lord?

With how much of our hearts must we search for Him?

At the beginning of verse 14, the Lord tells us what will happen as a result of this.

What does He declare?

Here in Jeremiah 29, God gave a warning to His people through the prophet Jeremiah. He warned them against listening to the prophets and diviners who were in their midst. He told them that He has not sent these prophets and diviners, and they should *not* listen to the dreams which they dream. He states very plainly in verse 9, "I have not sent them." Though the Lord is speaking to those in exile, I believe we can learn so much from these few verses. God wants us to seek Him, and He wants us to seek Him with our whole heart. And when we do that, He tells us that He will be found by us! What a precious promise. God doesn't play hide-and-seek. It isn't a game to Him. We don't have to find Him and then chase Him like we did with our friends when we played hide-and-seek as children. When we go looking for Him we truly find Him. The one condition is that we seek Him with all of our heart.

Do you want to know the plan He has for your life?

Look up Romans 8:29 to find out what it is. What did God predestine us to be?

Now stay in Romans 8 and read verses 28-31.

Through these verses you see that God has called you just as He called Paul. He does have a plan for your life. He predestined each of us to become conformed to the image of His Son. This is a *big* plan. I don't know about you, but for me to become conformed to the image of Christ takes some serious molding. I thank the Lord that He is the potter and that I am clay (see Isaiah 64:8), though sometimes I am more pliable than at other times. Can you relate? So, the Lord called us according to *His* purpose, He predestined us to become conformed to the image of His Son, He justified us, and He glorified us. What can we say? "If God is for us, who can be against us?" (Romans 8:31)

Once again, we have no excuses. It comes down to choices we make. We make choices either to seek Him and follow His plan for our lives or to follow our own plans and our own ways. In regard to obedience, neither you nor I would want Galatians 5:7 spoken of us: "You were running well; who hindered you from obeying the truth?"

If God asked you this question at this moment, what would your answer be?

God does have a plan for our lives. If you have a personal relationship with Him, then you are His child, you were called, and you have been set apart. Thankfully you now know what that plan is. His plan is for you and me to become conformed into the image of His Son. What is involved in becoming conformed to the image of Jesus Christ? A whole lot for sure! But each and every step is worth it, and you can bet that it takes a lot of obedience to the Lord! Do we know those steps along the way? Sometimes we do, but most of the time we don't. We do, however, know that when we follow His plan, great things happen for His kingdom. Read two verses from last week's lesson as we close:

"I am the vine, you are the branches; he who abides in Me and I in him, he bears much fruit, for apart from Me you can do nothing. . . . My Father is glorified by this, that you bear much fruit, and so prove to be My disciples."
John 15:5, 8

Simply stated, if we are abiding, then we will be obeying. And as we obey we bear fruit. It truly is a natural progression in the intimate Christian life. And then as I said, great things will happen for His kingdom because we will be bearing much fruit, and our heavenly Father will be glorified. Think of it like the following diagram:

Abiding→Obedience→Bearing Fruit→Kingdom Work→Father glorified!

Praise God for His truths! What an exciting truth this is. I pray His richest blessings on you for your desire to obey Him.

DAY 2: *Obedience Requires Dependence and Humility*

We are going to use the rest of the week to look at a very precious example of Jesus and His obedience. A couple of years ago, the Lord spoke to me through the following passage in such a mighty and powerful way that I have not been the same since. I learned so much from the Lord through the Holy Spirit's prompting. Actually the Lord used the things I learned in part to speak to me about writing this study on the example of Christ. I can hardly dig into this passage without becoming very emotional. I believe that we are given an extreme privilege to see this exchange between Jesus and His Father. Please prayerfully treat it as such. Pray and ask the Lord to give you divine wisdom as we learn from the example of Christ Jesus our Lord.

Read Matthew 26:36-46 slowly and prayerfully.

In the previous verses, Jesus has just told Peter that he (Peter) would deny Him three times before the rooster crows. Then Peter makes a bold statement by saying, "Even if I have to die with You, I will not deny You" (vs. 35). The Scripture then says that all the disciples said the same thing too. Poor Peter. I feel so sorry for him, because I can relate to him. There are things that I have said that I would never do (sometimes while criticizing another's actions) that I have then done. Even when we have the best of intentions, we still say things we shouldn't say and do things we shouldn't do. That is because we are human. That is why we all need a Savior. We need a Savior because, even with our best intentions and hearts set to do right, we still mess up. Thank you, Jesus, for doing exactly what You were sent to do!

In verse 37 the Scripture states that Jesus began to be what? ________________

and ________________________

Based on this insight, did Jesus know what was about to happen?

I want us to focus in on the next two verses today to make our points about Christ and the example He left for us to follow.

"Then He said to them, 'My soul is deeply grieved, to the point of death; remain here and keep watch with Me.' And He went a little beyond them, and fell on His face and prayed, saying, 'My Father, if it is possible, let this cup pass from Me; yet not as I will, but as You will.'"
Matthew 26:38-39

Obedience Requires Dependence

Jesus made a choice here that is important to see. Though we studied about prayer all last week, we will continue to see His example of prayer throughout this study.

Where did Jesus and His disciples go in verse 36?

What did He tell His disciples? (vs. 36)

At first whom did Jesus take with Him? (vs. 37)

We learn from Mark's account (Mark 14:33) that the two sons of Zebedee were James and John. What did Jesus say to Peter, James, and John? (vs. 38)

Then where did Jesus go?

Let's pause here to study Jesus' actions to this point. Jesus knew what lay ahead, yet what did Jesus do, knowing about the most difficult circumstances waiting before Him?

We can learn so much just from this one glimpse of Jesus' dependence upon the Father. He depended upon prayer so much that, rather than tell His crowd of disciples what was about to happen, or even the few who went farther with Him, He told God. When He was grieved and distressed He prayed to God. He went straight to God. He didn't discuss it with the disciples, fret over it, or worry about it. He went straight to the Father.

Remember how I asked you last week about where you run? Is it to the phone or the throne?

Have you tried to make a change since then?

We would be wise to learn from Christ that the first place to go is to the throne, no matter who you are with or what circumstances you face.

Now, let's examine these two verses again to make another very important point.

Obedience Requires Humility

"Then He said to them, 'My soul is deeply grieved, to the point of death; remain here and keep watch with Me.' And He went a little beyond them, and fell on His face and prayed, saying, 'My Father, if it is possible, let this cup pass from Me; yet not as I will, but as You will.'" Matthew 26:38-39

In verse 38 what did Jesus tell them about His soul?

Jesus' honesty and transparency with His disciples always touches me. Here He was the Son of God and He told them exactly and very frankly how He felt. He didn't go into all the details and pour His heart out to them, because that was meant for the Father to hear. However, it took humility to admit His feelings and emotions to His followers. He was the Son of God to them. Don't you think they looked to Him for security and strength?

After Jesus went a little beyond them, what did He do? (vs. 39) He __________________ on His _____________ and prayed.

Picture this and don't forget it. The scene is beautiful. Jesus fell on His face and prayed. I studied the phrase translated "fell on his face," and it means exactly that—He prostrated Himself face-first on the ground. The Son of God went flat out, to His face, in prayer to His Father. Read it and don't leave it until you get a mental picture.

Now I ask you to ask yourself the question that I gave you last week: If Jesus needs to fall on His face in prayer to the Lord, how much more should I?

This not only demonstrates humility in action, but to me it serves as an example of His desire to please the Father and His struggle to give over His own will to make it match the Father's will.

As Jesus was on His face before His Father, what did He pray to Him? (vs. 39)

Jesus asked in humility for a reprieve. In other words, if there was any way for this to not happen, then His desire would be that it didn't. Then He said, "Yet not as I will, but ____ ____." (vs. 39)

We will close with some personal application.

What really hard thing in your life have you failed to take to the Father in prayer? ______
____
____
____
____

Will you go to your face right now, give it to Him, and tell Him you desire His will above your own?

It may not be easy at first, but with His strength, you can do it. Obedience takes practice. Start now, and pour your heart out to Him. If it is hard for you, tell Him it is. He knows it all anyway. Ask Him to give you the dependence upon Him rather than on others.

O Father, make us as dependent on You as Your precious Son, Jesus, was. Let us learn from His example of humility, and may we be as willing to obey Your will above our own as He was. Amen.

DAY 3: *Obedience Requires Sacrifice and Perseverance*

Each time I begin a new day I am awed by Christ's example. As we study His each and every move in the Scripture, please don't forget that God wants to conform you into the image of His Son. All that we study about Jesus provides an example for us; it shows where we want to be someday. We want to be able to do what Jesus did. We want to depend upon the Father the way Christ did. We want to be humble before others and before our Lord as Jesus was. Thank God right now that we can learn so much from today's passage of Scripture. Ask Him to open your eyes to His Truth today.

Obedience Requires Sacrifice

Read Matthew 26:36-46 again and ask God to show you new and wonderful things (see Jeremiah 33:3). Today we will focus on four of the verses from this passage.

"And He took with Him Peter and the two sons of Zebedee, and began to be grieved and distressed. . . . And He went a little beyond them, and fell on His face and prayed, saying, 'My Father, if it is possible, let this cup pass from Me; yet not as I will, but as You will.'" Matthew 26:37, 39

We look again at verse 37 to realize that Jesus did indeed know what was coming. He knew what would be done to Him. That is why we can see such a struggle of His will. He foreknew every pain that would be felt and every sin that would rest upon His shoulders. He was sinless, and yet He would carry the sins of the world. Jesus sacrificed to obey.

He sacrificed all He was so that we could all be what we are today. Stop and write your prayer of thanksgiving to Him for what you are because of Him and what you will someday be because of Him. ____

____

____

____

____

Do not ever allow yourself to believe that Jesus didn't do this sacrificially. If you do, then you will rob yourself of the blessing of seeing His complete love and His perfect love for you. I know this is hard to believe. But it is so true. He does love you that much.

Is it hard for you to accept this kind of love?

Why?

Sometimes we have a hard time accepting pure, undefiled love. Love that isn't based upon our performance or on who we are is hard to accept because it isn't natural to give or receive this type of love. But God has that kind of love for you.

Read verse 39 again. Jesus said, "Not as I will, but as You will." Jesus told the Father that He was willing to sacrifice everything for the ultimate purpose—being your Savior and mine. God sent His Son, Jesus, to die for you, and His Son, Jesus, was willing to sacrifice Himself on your behalf. He was God in the flesh, and He felt as you and I feel—with emotions and feelings just like us. This was hard. This was sacrificial!

Now for personal application:

Do you sacrifice what you want to do for what God wants you to do?

In no way do the following examples compare with what Jesus did for us, but for the sake of examining our obedience consider the following questions. When God tells you to write a note to someone, pray for or with someone, take a meal to someone, make time for a family member, or give up something, do you do it?

Do you do it right when He tells you to or when it is convenient for you?

Is your obedience based on whether you feel like doing it or not?

Sometimes the things God asks us to do take time, and sometimes that is the one thing we are most selfish with—our time. Sometimes we give money more readily than our time. Have you been guilty of that?

No matter how we sugarcoat it, partial obedience is disobedience.

Read 1 Samuel 15:16-23. Here you will see how God called the prophet Samuel to share a message from God with Saul.

See verses 20-21. Saul was basically saying, "I did obey the **Lord** except for this, that, and the other. And my disobedience was for a sacrifice (burnt offerings) to the Lord." Saul was justifying his partial obedience. He had not done what God had said to do. He had done what he wanted to do and what he thought was best. Then the prophet Samuel told Saul what God thought about his partial obedience. Look at the Lord's reply through Samuel in verses 22-23.

You see, Saul was justifying his actions by saying, "But we took these things so that they could be used as a burnt offering to the Lord." Please don't confuse the two words for sacrifice here. The sacrifice Saul spoke of was a burnt offering; the kind of sacrifice that I speak of—Jesus' example—is giving up our will for His. Have you been like Saul and been guilty of doing things that God has told you to do and doing them only halfway?

Maybe it was doing them up to the point of comfort and then you left the rest undone. Obedience takes sacrifice. It demands that we give up our will for His will. It requires a desire to follow His will more than our own. Don't deceive yourself; it wasn't easy for Jesus to go to the cross. Nor was it easy for His Father to send Him to the cross on our behalf. It was a sacrifice!

Stop now and listen to the Lord. What has He told you to do in the past that you haven't done? Write it out and then pray to Him and tell Him to give you the courage, dependence, and humility to do it. Then ask Him for forgiveness for failing to obey Him fully. ______________

____

____

____

____

You may not know all the ways in which you have failed to obey the Lord. The previous question may be a difficult one for you. However, if you ask the Lord to show you where and how you have been disobedient, He will be faithful to answer. You must be willing to listen and persevere in order to obey.

Obedience Requires Perseverance

Jesus told His disciples:

> ***"'Keep watching and praying that you may not enter into temptation; the spirit is willing, but the flesh is weak.' He went away again a second time and prayed, saying, 'My Father, if this cannot pass away unless I drink it, Your will be done.' . . . And He left them again, and went away and prayed a third time, saying the same thing once more." Matthew 26:41-42, 44***

In verse 41 Jesus told the disciples to "keep watching and praying, that you may not enter into temptation; the spirit is willing, but the flesh is weak." Jesus knows that the enemy—and our own desires to satisfy self—will do everything possible to keep you from obeying. This provides yet another example of the war of the flesh and spirit, which we will study more in our week on temptation. Jesus displayed for us in these verses His perseverance to obey. Don't you think that when Jesus stated, "the spirit is willing, but the flesh is weak" that He was experiencing this Himself? Because He was God, though He came in the form of man with a mind, emotions, and will like ours, He knew what He was capable of doing or not doing.

Read verses 42 and 44 again. I believe Jesus kept entreating the Father for His strength, power, direction, and for the Father's will to be done above His own. He knew without divine ability, He would not be able to do this. He knew He must keep going to God.

The question again: If Jesus needed to persevere and entreat God over and over to obey, how much more should I?

Is there anything you have stopped praying about because you felt like you have asked too often or because you have given up since you haven't seen an answer? If so, what is it? ____

____

____

____

____

Trust God with it now, ask Him again, and ask Him to forgive your lack of faith.

God desires for us to go to Him in prayer about everything, and He doesn't get tired of hearing us ask the same thing over and over, especially if it is in perseverance to obey Him!

DAY 4: *Obedience Requires Trust and Faith*

So far we have studied Jesus' dependence, humility, sacrifice, and perseverance. Today we will look at the faith and trust He displayed through His obedience. We will add a few more verses to the passage in Matthew 26. Please pray for God to give you a very sensitive spirit and fresh perspective to these Scriptures. Read the following verses:

"Then He came to the disciples and said to them, 'Are you still sleeping and resting? Behold, the hour is at hand and the Son of Man is being betrayed into the hands of sinners. Get up, let us be going; behold, the one who betrays Me is at hand!' . . . Then Jesus said to him, 'Put your sword back into its place; for all those who take up the sword shall perish by the sword. Or do you think that I cannot appeal to My Father, and He will at once put at My disposal more than twelve legions of angels? How then will the Scriptures be fulfilled, which say that it must happen this way?' At that time Jesus said to the crowds, 'Have you come out with swords and clubs to arrest Me as you would against a robber? Every day I used to sit in the temple teaching and you did not seize Me. But all this has taken place to fulfill the Scriptures of the prophets.' Then all

the disciples left Him and fled." Matthew 26:45-46, 52-56

We have established that Jesus knew what was coming. Now the time had come. He accepted what He had been called to do and obeyed His Father. How could Jesus be so obedient? Because He trusted in His Father's will. Notice how Jesus sets them straight about who is in control in verse 53.

What did Jesus say that He could do?

Do you believe that?

Jesus could have had twelve legions of angels come to His rescue, but instead He desired to do His Father's will above all else. He knew His Father's plan involved Him going to the cross to fulfill Scripture (vs. 54). You and I can experience this depth of commitment to obey our Father as well. We must trust in God's power and have faith in God's plans and His ways. Remember Isaiah 55:8-9, "'For My thoughts are not your thoughts, nor are your ways My ways,' declares the LORD. 'For as the heavens are higher than the earth, so are My ways higher than your ways and My thoughts than your thoughts.'" He does have a plan for us. We must trust and have faith in His plan and believe His ways are better than any way or plan we could ever come up with. Even when we don't understand or can't see the entire puzzle of our life in place, we still must trust. Since we can't even begin to understand or comprehend His plans and His ways, wouldn't we be better off trusting? However, God doesn't leave us with our attitude of, "Oh well, I'll just trust Him because I should." No, God gives us Truth straight from His Word so that we know that we know that we can and should trust Him.

Believing a very important truth about His character can help you to trust in Him. He is El Elyon, the God Most High. He first revealed Himself as El Elyon in Genesis 14:17-24. Through His names we learn His character. This name essentially means that He is sovereign and that He is in control of all things.

Read Isaiah 14:24, 27.

Does what God intends or plans happen?

Can anyone or anything change or mess up His plans?

Nothing can thwart the plan of God! And we do know that God has plans. Nothing takes Him by surprise when it happens. He knew before we knew what we would do. He knew before any and every disaster that it would happen. This is the truth that literally set me free from so much fear and anxiety many years ago. Nothing happens to you or me without God allowing it or causing it to happen. To rest in this truth makes the difference between a peaceful, trusting life and a life full of anxiety and fear. I will always choose peace and trust over anxiety and fear! If you have a hard time believing this truth from Scripture, would you tell God about it? Would you pour your heart out to Him and let Him know that you struggle with this, yet desire for Him to make His truth known deep within your soul?

Before we close today, I have to show you something that is so precious that I don't want you to miss the blessing. Go back to our Scripture in Matthew 26. In verse 45 Jesus goes to the disciples once more and finds them sleeping. He says to them, "Behold, the hour is at hand and the Son of Man is being betrayed into the hands of sinners." Just prior to this in verse 42, we see that Jesus had approached the Father praying once more, "My Father, if this cannot pass away unless I drink it, Your will be done." As we have seen, this was His third time to pray this same prayer. We have looked at His perseverance during this time. He persevered so that He could obey. However, don't miss what happened between His persevering and His obeying vss. 44-45). Although I can only imagine what that moment was like for Christ, I know how it feels for myself because I am so familiar with that poignant place in-between that point of surrender. Jesus surrendered. Let me say it again. Jesus Christ, the Son of God, surrendered to His Father's will above His own. After He prayed a third time for God's will above His own, He accepted what must be done and acknowledged the time had come. When we face a call to obedience, we make a choice: to obey or not to obey. Though the statement sounds simple, we know it isn't simple at all. As we have learned from Christ, we can ask to be given a reprieve or we can persevere and pray fervently for the desire and courage to obey. However, no matter what we do when we are called to obey, at some point we come to the crossroads of surrendering or standing against His command. To stand against His will is to deny His lordship in our lives. To surrender is to submit. Surrender is precious. Jesus chose surrender. I hope that you have experienced enough times of surrender that you want to keep surrendering to experience the peace that comes from it.

Surrender→ Obedience→ Peace

Enjoy the following gift that the Lord gave me as His encouragement to both of us:

Surrender

Surrender, Father, is what I desire to do,
To fall on my face in submission to You.
Precious, sweet surrender is the voice I hear
When I need You to take over and make it for real.
I can't hold on any longer, my desire I must pry,
My will is not the best, so why do I lie?
I listen to my heart and then my head,
Believing that my way is better instead.
What a false sense of being this is to me.
If I've lived it so often, why aren't I free?

To trust, obey sooner, to come to the peak;
I look over the edge, and You I seek.
Though I don't see Your plan, it is You I trust
To carry me through and provide, yes, You must.
You have promised it to me in Your Word,
Never unfaithful is what I have heard.

Father, Yours is the voice that I continue to hear,
"Run to Me child, Your life I hold dear.
Give up this fight and struggle once again.
To have your way and not Mine, is not a win."

I know, sweet Father, Your way is always best;
Somehow, some way, in this I will rest.
I give up my will to trust and obey,
Now give me the courage to follow Your way.
I submit and surrender, to You I will give
My all and all, so like Jesus I may live.

Surrender is precious, and like Jesus I will be
When I fall on my face in submission to Thee.

Lori Merrill
My prayer to my Father
January 17, 2003

Surrender comes at the very moment we choose His way. The mind is made up, thus the burden is lifted. The Holy Spirit is given control. The flesh has died. There is almost no other feeling like it—knowing the flesh has submitted to the Spirit. (We will talk more about this while studying temptation.) Tomorrow I will share with you some very personal ways in which I have been called to surrender.

How has God spoken to you today? What has He called you to do that you haven't surrendered to? Stop and listen to Him, for He will answer. ______________________________

____

____

____

____

____

I am praying that you will not miss one word that He tells you! God bless!

DAY 5: *Do You Have Peace and Contentment?*

How many times have you said "ouch" this week? Obedience—it is just one of those subjects, isn't it? If you have already said "ouch" this week, then get one more really loud "OUCH" in before you continue. Okay, are we ready to begin? Yesterday's lesson was hard; in fact, this whole week has been hard. Obedience is always hard at first, but the more we do it the better we get at it. I once heard it said that if we don't teach our children to obey us, then how would we expect them to obey God? That has stayed with me—much to my children's chagrin—ever since I became a parent, because of course I want my children to love God and obey Him fully! My parents cornered the market on obedience. I never wanted to have an appointment with the belt or the flyswatter. Yes, I did say flyswatter. Still to this day I empathize with flies as I chase them with the swatter. I was scared to death to disobey my parents because of the wrath that would follow! Of course, we want our children to obey out of love and not fear, just as the Father desires that for us. But for me, I have made it clear to the Lord that if He has to put fear in me because love doesn't come out of me first—so be it. He has my permission, though I know He doesn't need it.

I do love to obey Him. I love to receive hard assignments from Him so I can obey Him more. I cannot explain all the joy and satisfaction that comes from obeying. You just have to experience it! I am not saying obedience is always fun, because it isn't. But it does produce Christlike characteristics in me, and that is always worth it! Why is obedience so important to me? Let me list a few reasons:

1. **Obedience is important to God.**
   God uses obedience to grow us and to continue to conform us into the image of His Son. Without obedience we can become stagnant in our walk and dry in our times with Him. I have heard it said often that if you experience a dry time with the Lord, then look back over your life and see when you last told God no. That point when you told God no is likely when you broke fellowship with Him and the well began to be dry.

2. **Disobedience is a sin.**
   Read James 4:17 and fill in the blanks.

   "Therefore, to one who _______________ the ______________ thing to do and does not do it, to him it is _____________________." So, when God prompts us to do something and we ignore that prompting, we are disobeying, thus sinning against God. That statement alone makes me want to be a better listener so that I don't miss a single command!

3. **Obedience produces fruit.**
   Obedience to God is God working out His glory through us, and it results in kingdom work. God does great things through His people and works miracles through us when we obey. Does He need us to display His glory? No, He displays His glory all throughout creation, but He chooses to use us as well.

   Look up Isaiah 43:7 and tell me why we were created.

   As you can see, when we obey Him, we bring more honor and glory to Him. Obedience doesn't point others to us; it points them to God.

4. **Obedience pleases the Father.**
   I think this is the prime reason for me. I want to please the Father, and I am sure you do too or you wouldn't be doing this study. I love the peace and contentment which come from pleasing the Father. That point of surrender may seem hard to reach, but once there you experience true relief. This kind of relief is far better than anything a TUMS® or Rolaids® could do for you! Read the following verses and ask God to help you examine your life as He does. Write in your own words what these verses say.

   Galatians 1:10

   Acts 5:29

Sometimes it does us good to examine ourselves to see whom we are obeying and the motives behind our obedience. We want our motives to be pure. Of course, we want to obey God rather than men. There have been times in my life that I have had to carry Galatians 1:10 around with me on an index card. I have even had to carry it to a few church meetings and place it right in front of me! Why? Because there definitely have been times when I find myself desiring to be accepted and liked, moments that I have been tempted to be a man- or woman-pleaser more than a pleaser of my Lord. I am embarrassed to admit that to you, but my insecurities have sometimes come close to taking over and making it difficult for me to stand firm as I should. It grieves my heart when I look back over the occasions that a person's approval was more important than God's approval in my life. One of my regular prayers for my children is Luke 2:52—"Jesus kept increasing in wisdom and stature, and in favor with God and men." I pray that for my children; however, though I want them to enjoy favor with men, I want them to stand in favor with God first. Many times you can't have both! If we choose to obey God, then there will be times that we are out of favor with men. God does tell us in His Word to submit to authorities and leaders, and this pleases Him. The only time we should not submit is if following their rules places us in opposition to God's laws.

Write about a time when you chose to please others rather than to please God? ________
____
____
____

Be sure to ask God to forgive you for this and to do what He has to so you don't fall into this temptation again.

At times, God asks or requires things of us that others don't understand. Sometimes He wants others to know the testimony that this brings, and other times these are just things meant to be between you and the Lord. I remember when God prompted me to give up my cell phone once. This was just one of those times that it was "our little secret." I can remember the relief I felt the first time I could afford a cell phone. The relief was because of fear. For a multitude of reasons, I was a very fearful person, especially when it came to driving anywhere alone or with my three young children. I remember feeling the security of a cell phone, the assurance that if anything happened to me I would be safe. Until one day God prompted me with the question, "Am I your security or is the cell phone?" and with another question, "Do you believe and trust in my sovereignty?" You see, I had learned that God is my El Elyon—the God Most High. His character, shown through this name, states that He is Sovereign and in control of *all* things. If I believed this, then why would a cell phone make me feel better? God called me on the carpet, so to speak. If I really believed this, then why didn't I live it? So, with much prayer and anticipation, I told my husband to cancel the cell phone. This was a real growing experience for me. Everywhere I went I had to travel the interstate, so whether I faced a long or short trip, I prayed for God to be my safety and my stronghold and to give me peace and rest while driving. He did, and since I was depending on Him, I grew in my faith and trust in Him. I do have a cell phone today, so don't think I am against cell phones, but I didn't get one until I had permission from the Lord—which took about a year. I don't know if you can relate to that kind of fear, but we all have things that we hold on to instead of holding to Him.

Will you spend a few minutes listening to Him and hearing what He might want you to give up to trust Him more?

Now pray for the desire to obey.

Sometimes obedience doesn't require such introspection. Sometimes it simply means following through on a thought or prompting. Once God prompted me during my prayer time to give away something that I really enjoyed. I was praying for a friend with cancer. During my prayer for her, the Lord reminded me of a CD of mine that truly ministered to me. There are two songs on this particular CD that the Lord has used many times over to minister to me and sometimes to others as I have shared them during the Bible studies I teach. Well, at first I dismissed this prompting as "my idea." Then, as the Lord kept reminding me of how blessed I have been by the words of one particular song, I relented. I agreed I would continue to pray about it and make sure it came from Him and see how He wanted me to go about giving this away. Over the next two weeks before doing this, I thought of many things. First I went to the store to try to buy it, though I thought it was unlikely I would find it. It was. It was too old and no longer available (remember, this was before iTunes). I thought about what I would say. Many doubts came to mind during this time, such as: "The CD case is cracked and broken so it doesn't look nice—how embarrassing;" "She probably has it already;" and "What if it isn't You, Lord, saying this—how stupid will I look giving a very used gift?" Then I realized that I, in my selfishness, wouldn't willingly want to give away my favorite CD, so this had to be from Him. I would trust and obey! So I did. I wrote my friend a note explaining that the Lord told me to do this and that there were two songs I needed her to listen to. I told her I hoped that they would truly minister to her as they had to me. I left it for her and didn't hear from her for two weeks. When I was tempted to feel foolish, I reminded myself that the important thing was that I had obeyed and the Lord knew my heart. I knew I would rather be a fool for Him than fail to obey! One day after church she walked up to me and with tears in her eyes said, "You don't know how God has used those songs to minister to me. Thank you so much." We hugged and both cried. I told her I was sorry I had delayed, but was so glad I had obeyed. As I told my family the story in the car, I boohooed! I had been so reluctant and selfish, but what joy that surrender had brought!

Read Philippians 4:6-7 below and answer the questions.

"Be anxious for nothing, but in everything by prayer and supplication with thanksgiving let your requests be made known to God. And the peace of God, which surpasses all comprehension, will guard your hearts and your minds in Christ Jesus."

Whose peace is it?

Can we understand it?

Can we have it?

How?

What will this peace do for us?

My obedience brought joy, and that joy brought peace and contentment. There is a peace that we can't attain to or gain from this world, nor do we understand it. It is the peace that surpasses all understanding. I'm sure you know from your own personal experiences what this peace and contentment feels like. If we want to get used to hearing His voice, His call to obedience, then we must practice obeying Him swiftly and quickly. The result will be kingdom work done through us by Him, and joy for us as well—the joy that results in peace and contentment because we know we are pleasing Him.

I share these stories with you to give you a glimpse of what obedience sometimes looks like. These stories relate some of my easier assignments from God, yet they are just as important as any other. I wouldn't have ever been faced with obedience had I not been in prayer. I could not have been obedient without relying on the Lord in prayer. And I certainly wouldn't have the peace and contentment that obedience brings had I not obeyed Him fully. Obedience becomes more difficult when it involves calls to confront others, love others, and forgive others who have hurt you. However, it takes obedience in the small things to prepare us for obedience in the more difficult tasks. God tells us in His Word that He who is faithful in a very little thing will be faithful in much (see Luke 16:10). Begin now to obey Him in even the little things so that you will be ready to obey Him when the harder things come along.

Let's close this week with one more look at Jesus' perfect example for us. Read the verse and then ask God to show you how to be more like His Son.

"Although He was a Son, He learned obedience from the things which He suffered." Hebrews 5:8

Write your prayer to Him, date it, and then pray daily for a sensitive heart to hear clearly as God calls. I am praying for you. Praise God for His Son's obedience that saved us!

Week 3

Jesus: His Example of Facing Temptation

"For we do not have a high priest who cannot sympathize with our weaknesses, but One who has been tempted in all things as we are, yet without sin." Hebrews 4:15

Day 1
Enemy Alert!

Day 2
Wilderness Experiences

Day 3
Standing Firm

Day 4
We Are Not Alone

Day 5
Flesh vs. Spirit

Memory and Meditation Verse: "But I say, walk by the Spirit, and you will not carry out the desire of the flesh." Galatians 5:16

Prayer: *Precious heavenly Father, we praise Your holy name. You indeed are holy and pure. Father, I ask that You awaken us to the temptations all around us each and every day. Lord, give us new eyes to see those areas where we are weak and so very vulnerable because we have never given them over to You. I pray for us to be aware of the power that is available to us through Your Spirit, Father. Make us willing vessels to be used by You and help us to learn from Your Son by how He faced temptation and yet was without sin. Lord, teach us to live by the Spirit rather than the lust of the flesh. Thank you for teaching us all these things so that we may continue to be conformed to the image of Your Son.* **Amen.**

Week 3

Jesus: His Example of Facing Temptation

"For we do not have a high priest who cannot sympathize with our weaknesses, but One who has been tempted in all things as we are, yet without sin." Hebrews 4:15

Day 1: Enemy Alert!

This week we will study Christ's example of facing temptation. This is one subject I think we tend to give little thought to. Yet I have learned that being aware of our tendency to sin when faced with temptation makes us more aware when the temptation comes our way. If we really examine the process of what we go through when tempted, I truly believe we are less likely to sin. We are less likely to sin because we have been made aware that at that very moment we stand at a crossroad of choices. Just as I stated in last week's lesson, we make the choice to obey or not to obey. This week we will examine how at that crossroad point we make the same choice to follow the Spirit or follow our flesh. It is interesting for sure. We will study it intently so you understand what I mean. Jesus left us an example to follow so that we would know how to follow the Spirit as He did. Once again we will begin this week by taking a peek into His life experience; this time it is His wilderness experience. To establish the context of our passage this week, please read Mark 1:9-13 and answer the following questions:

What had just happened to Jesus?

What had the Father said to Him?

Then where did He go?

Why?

How soon after Jesus was baptized did this happen?

How long was He there? (vs. 13) _____ days being __________________ by Satan

Let us first look at this word *impelled*. It means "to drive out, cast out," and in the NIV the words used for impelled are "sent out." I found it interesting that the definitions of this word all state "to be driven out, in a stern though not violent way." Also, the *Strong's Lexicon* stated, "Of the world, i.e., be deprived of the power and influence he exercises in the world."[7] In other words, the Spirit "so strongly urged" Jesus to go into the wilderness, and He went.

At first I had thought we would begin our study by looking at how Jesus was tempted and examining each temptation. However, very quickly the Lord prompted me to change directions to focus on the *tempter* first. He reminded me of the importance of knowing our enemy and his tactics in order for us to be able to engage in war with him. Just as a country does not go to war without knowing and trying to understand their enemies, we have to be fully informed as well. The more we understand about Satan, the more we will know how to stand against him. I am not in any way promoting a study of Satan; however, we cannot remain ignorant of him either.

Please read Luke 4:1-13 and answer the questions below.

What had the devil finished? (vs. 13)

Why did the devil leave Him?

The devil left Jesus until an opportune time. I hope this speaks volumes to you about Satan and his tactics. It does to me. Be very aware that Satan and his host of demons *do not give up*! They may not succeed at first, but as the saying goes, they will "try and try again!" Satan, even after failing to cause Christ to stumble, had every intention of going back for more. He would just wait until another time. To learn more about this enemy we call the Devil, look up 1 Peter 5:8 and fill in the blanks.

"Be of sober spirit, be on the alert. Your______________________, the devil, _________________________ around like a roaring lion, seeking someone to ___________________________."

If you have made the assumption that Satan is not alive and active in this world, then you, my friend, are mistaken. If you have not given much thought to him and his host of demons, then may I lovingly tell you that he has you right where he wants you. This verse is only one of many that warn us of our enemy and his war against us. Please do not play into his scheme by refusing to believe that he has a plan for you too. This may be uncomfortable for you to think about, but please stay with me for a few more minutes and be willing to squirm. His plan is everything opposite of the Father's plan. As you learned last week, God does have a plan for your life—one that is for good, not for calamity, one that gives you a future and a hope (see Jeremiah 29:11).

Let's pick apart this verse in 1 Peter to understand and unearth all the treasure hidden within its context.

"Be of sober spirit, be on the alert"—I want to first draw your attention to the word *alert*. This word means "to be watchful, to give strict attention to, cautious." Notice that this sentence stops right there. Before going any further, we have been told to be of sober spirit (self-controlled), to be on the alert. We have to be self-controlled, to remain watchful and cautious. We have to always know in our mind that Satan is out there scheming, planning an attack, watching us. If we don't constantly realize this, we can easily become sluggish and unprepared. Then, before we realize what has happened, we have had a surprise attack that we were not ready for. Many times this has been the worst kind of attack for me. I am in way too far before I realize that I have been caught off guard. That is why we are commanded, not just warned, to be on the alert. We also must stay alert because one of Satan's many tactics, I have learned, is to wear us down so that we grow weary, battered, and bruised from the war that is being waged against us. Sometimes he plans such an onslaught of attacks—one after another—that we grow so weary of the battle we are tempted to give in or give up!

We also have to remain alert because sometimes the opposite is true. We become comfortable in our life and our Christian walk and think that all is fine. Things go so well for a while that we let our guard down. Then we become easy prey. Before I go on with this thought, may I suggest to you something that may sound radical? If your life as a Christian is a very easy, comfortable life without hardship, struggle, or pain, then I would challenge you to ask the Lord what kind of impact you are making for His kingdom. The reason I suggest this is because I believe that if you are not a threat to Satan's plan of destruction, then he will leave you alone. I am not saying that every Christian lives a martyred life, but please give the previous suggestion some prayerful thought. Now let's get back to our look into being on the alert. Read Ephesians 6:10-11 and then answer the following questions:

Who are we to be strong in?

Whose strength are we to rely on?

What are we to put on?

What are we to stand firm against?

Now read verse 12 in the same chapter. List below all the things that our struggle is and is not against.

Struggles

Not against	**Against**

Where are these struggles taking place? ____

You see, God does make clear to us that a war is raging, and it is raging in the heavenly places. Satan is against us, and he is powerful, though not even close to a match for our Lord. However, we have a responsibility. That responsibility is to be educated in God's Word and to abide in Him so that we are able to do what verse 13 states. Read it below:

Therefore, take up the full armor of God, so that you will be able to resist in the evil day, and having done everything, to stand firm. *(NIV)*

I don't think Scripture gets much clearer than that. We are to rely on God's strength and to be strong in Him. We are to put on the full armor of God so that we can resist and stand firm against the schemes of the devil. For now, let's continue our look at 1 Peter 5:8:

"Be of sober spirit, be on the alert. Your adversary, the devil, prowls around like a roaring lion, seeking someone to devour." (NIV)

"Your adversary, the devil"—Why do we need to remain alert? The next sentence tells us. Our adversary (which means our enemy or opponent), the Devil, prowls around like a lion. We are given a very visual picture here so that we can understand exactly what Satan is like. He is our enemy, and he prowls around. This word for "prowls around" means "to walk, to progress, to make due use of opportunities." You see, he is looking for that opportunity all the time, just as he left Jesus until an opportune time. He doesn't have the advantage of being all-knowing, sovereign, and in control. He only has dominion to a point, and that point is chosen by God. However, he does watch us, keep an eye on us, and stalk us. In fact, he keeps such an eye on us that he knows our weaknesses and where and how we are vulnerable. How does he know that? Not because he is all-knowing, but because he is that crafty. He has studied us, baited us, and knows what works against us, as well as where we are susceptible to sin.

"Prowls around like a roaring lion"—Think about a lion and how he paces back and forth. Also, allow yourself to think about a lion that lies in wait to capture his prey. When you picture this lion sneaking, stalking, hiding, crouching—you are picturing your enemy doing the same thing. What enemy comes forth in the open to capture you and take you captive? None. An enemy has a plan and lies in wait until just the right time, an "opportune time." I once heard a pastor say that he asked the local zookeeper about a lion and why he roars. The answer was simple: He roars when he is hungry. What a picture that is for us. Our enemy is indeed hungry. Satan knows his time is limited and then the battle is over (John 12:31, John 16:11, 1 John 5:19, Revelation 12:12). His plan, his job, is to take as many of God's creatures down with him as possible. There is no hope of him winning, so the next best thing is to grieve the heart of God by deceiving as many as he can and making them believe that all this world has to offer is better than anything the Lord could offer.

"Seeking someone to devour"—He will take anyone he can get. It doesn't matter if it is one who is deceived and doesn't know the Lord or one of our brothers and sisters in Christ. His plan is to keep them deceived and/or living an unfulfilled life. I used to wonder why he would go after Christians since there is no hope of us being taken from our future eternity. But I have learned that Satan can use one of God's children in mighty ways to attempt to destroy the testimony of the Lord. In other words, if he can take a known Christian down a path of destruction, then how many potential Christians does he take with him? These may be people who may have someday called on God as their Savior, yet because of a testimony ruined, will vow to have nothing to do with Christianity and what it represents to them. Oh, Satan is hungry and he is seeking whomever he can devour. This word *devour* is interesting as well. It means "to destroy, to swallow up." You see, he doesn't desire to just hurt us—though that is good to him—but he wants to completely destroy us! He doesn't want to just take a bite either; rather, his plan of action is to swallow us up in one gulp. Scary? It can be, but we can't *let* it be. We have a God whose name is El Elyon, our God Most High. You can be sure that He is in complete control. Satan can't make us sin; we choose that ourselves. Can he tempt? Yes. Can he set traps and snares to make us stumble? Yes, but we are not *forced* to do anything. We still have choices. This is why it is so important to be watchful, alert, and cautious. We have to stand firm!

Have you been obedient to be "alert" as 1 Peter 5:8 tells us to be?

If not, then write your prayer to the Lord, confessing your lack of attentiveness, and ask Him to teach you to how to stand firm. ____

My desire here is to make each of us more aware. We cannot go blindly into this battle; it is important to know what we are up against. I pray this has given you a clearer picture also of what Christ was up against. We will delve into that tomorrow. For now, thank our Lord that we have His Son's example to follow.

DAY 2: *Wilderness Experiences*

Yesterday we learned about our enemy. We became a little more educated about who he is and what he does. Today we will study a little more about him and his plans, his ways, and his schemes. We will look to Christ's personal experience with Satan and how He handled it. To do this we will examine Jesus' personal wilderness experience. Although we will look into how Satan tempted Him, we want our focus to be on how Jesus is our example while facing temptation. There are two places in the New Testament that give the details of this temptation. Yesterday you read Luke's version, and today we will look at Matthew's account.

Read Matthew 4:1-11.

From this passage, how many times did Satan go to Jesus to tempt Him?

Notice that Satan used three different approaches to entice Christ to sin. Let's look at these three tactics so that we can see what he uses with us as well.

1. **Satan will attempt to place doubt.**

Notice Satan's statements in verses 3 and 6 below.

"And the tempter came and said to Him, 'If You are the Son of God, command that these stones become bread.'" (vs. 3)

"If You are the Son of God, throw Yourself down; for it is written, 'He will command His angels concerning You;' and 'On* their *hands they will bear You up, so that You will not strike Your foot against a stone.'" (vs. 6)

What word do both of these questions begin with?

With what seven words does Satan begin both of his statements to Jesus?

One of Satan's strongest weapons is doubt. Whether we realize it or not, you and I face it all the time. Whether he uses our hidden insecurities, circumstances, or people to promote the doubt, it doesn't really matter. He loves to make us doubt who we are. His statements to Christ were a challenge. In essence, Satan was saying to Jesus, "Since you are the Son of God, then . . ." It brings a mental picture of a playground bully to my mind saying, "Oh yeah, well then prove it!" As anyone who has heard those words knows, they instantly invoke pride within each of us. Someone who doubts our abilities, who we are, or what we can do, and then states "prove it" has just dared us to prove them wrong. This taunt wells up within us an incredible desire to "strut our stuff." Satan was appealing to a common downfall in all of us: pride. Thank God that Jesus had none of it. Read just a few verses from God's Word on the subject of pride below.

"When pride comes, then comes dishonor,
But with the humble is wisdom."
Proverbs 11:2

"Pride goes before destruction,
and a haughty spirit before stumbling."
Proverbs 16:18

"For all that is in the world, the lust of the flesh and the lust of the eyes and
the boastful pride of life, is not from the Father, but is from the world."
1 John 2:16

Pride. Unfortunately as Christians, we can't live with it, and we can't live without it (almost)! It is just one of those characteristics that the moment we think it is under control, we see more come to the surface. Knowing who we are in Christ is so very important to each of us as it helps prevent pride from ruling our lives. It is easy to fall into this entrapment if we are not secure with who we are. I am not talking about a healthy self-esteem; I am talking about a healthy God-esteem. You see, when we are secure with who we are because of the Lord and not because of our capabilities or achievements, then we will not become puffed up. We need to fully realize that anything that we are is because of what Christ did for us. It is God who works in us through the power of the Holy Spirit to conform us into the image of His Son. Anything good in us is because God lives within us!

Jesus didn't succumb to Satan's dare of "if You are, then You will do this." Jesus knew exactly who He was. Better than that, He knew He had nothing to prove—especially to this evil foe. Even with all the power that Jesus had at His disposal, the temptation to prove exactly who He was or to display His power didn't make Him sin. Please realize that Jesus had the power to take the challenge at that very moment, however, also realize that any time we rise to a challenge such as this, we are being lured into a pride trap by Satan.

Can you think of something in your life (a person or a situation) that invokes pride within you?

Please give this person or situation to the Lord, and let Him deal with you concerning it. Write your prayer to Him now, and remember that if it weren't for doubt about yourself, you wouldn't feel such a need to "prove it." ______________________________

2. **Satan will offer to provide immediate relief and comfort.**
Have you ever noticed how in our times of distress Satan always has a great plan to help us? Just as Satan had a great plan for Eve in the Garden of Eden, he will try to sell you his modern-day plan as well. He will try to show you all the benefits—without any of the drawbacks—of the deal. He reminds me of a very smooth and cunning salesman. The problem is that while we normally might not listen to the plan, when we are in the midst of a trial or difficulty, any escape can look very appealing. It is sad, isn't it? Look at how He tempted Jesus to take Him out of His level of discomfort.

Read again Matthew 4:1-3.

How long had Jesus fasted?

What was His physical state of being?

What did the tempter challenge Him to do?

Would this have relieved Jesus of His discomfort?

Giving in certainly would have relieved Jesus of His hunger; however, that was not God's plan for His Son. Jesus knew to follow His Father's plan and not to take any of Satan's deals along the way.

Can you think of a time when you were going through a difficult circumstance and the enemy offered you a "better deal"?

Did you take it?

How did you feel afterward?

No matter how good one of Satan's plans looks at the time, we must trust God and listen to what we know from our head rather than our heart.

Look up Jeremiah 17:9 and fill in the blanks below.

"The heart is more ____________________ than all else and is desperately ______________________."

Discomfort (physical, emotional, or spiritual) can make us lose perspective and make it difficult for us to distinguish between God's plan and Satan's scheme. That is why abiding is so important. It is at these times that we certainly can't rely on feelings (our heart); we must rely on God! We must keep our focus on eternal things and not on our temporary surroundings or solutions. If the solution is Satan's, then you can bet it will only provide temporary relief! However, the negative consequences of taking that relief will far outweigh any suffering that we were experiencing because of Christ. Suffering for Jesus produces eternal results. This kind of suffering is worth much more than any temporary relief.

3. **Satan will appeal to a vulnerability or weakness within us.**
Satan tried to appeal to Jesus by offering Him control over the world and all its riches and powers. Read Matthew 4:8-9 below.

"Again, the devil took Him to a very high mountain and showed Him all the kingdoms of the world and their glory; and he said to Him, 'All these things I will give You, if You fall down and worship me.'"

A couple of things strike me as interesting in this statement that the Devil made to Jesus. The first is that I believe he was trying to find a weak point in Jesus. Not only do you and I have pressure points on our bodies where if the right amount of pressure is applied we may faint or pass out, but we also have similar pressure points or weak points in our lives. This area is a vulnerability or weak tendency toward certain sins. It may be because of the way we were raised, an insecurity, something we once adored, or the hope of something we desire to be. No matter what it is, I believe that because of these vulnerabilities within us, if we do not guard against exposure to constant temptation, we will likely fail.

Don't think for a moment that Satan hasn't watched you closely enough to find your weak areas. The temptations that he provides and that work are the ones he will keep pounding you with. Let's just say it this way: Satan keeps a close eye on our vulnerabilities so he knows where to aim his fiery dart.

The second thing that is important to note in the Devil's statement is what Satan wanted Jesus to do in exchange for the power, riches, and glory he was offering.

In verse 9 what did Satan want Jesus to do?

"All these things I will give You if You __________ __________ and _______________ me."

The very reason Satan was banned and cast out of heaven is because of what he wanted to be and do. Here we see he was still trying to accomplish this with Jesus. He wants to be God. He wants to be higher than God. He wants to be worshiped like God. He wants this so much that He tried to get the Son of God to worship him. It is so ironic and yet so pitiful.

Unfortunately, I can relate too well to worshiping something other than my Lord. I am ashamed to say that there have been times in my life when the pursuit of possessions, money, time, comfort, glory, my desires, and the like was more important than the pursuit of the Lord was to me.

What about you? Will you be like Jesus and refuse to worship anything other than your precious heavenly Father?

List some things that you have pursued or are pursuing right now that may seem more important than your pursuit to worship only Him.

Now give that list to God. Ask His forgiveness, and ask Him to enable you to be aware immediately when you start pursuing these "things" more than you pursue Him. Thank Him now for His patience with you.

DAY 3: *Standing Firm*

With everything we have learned about our enemy, I pray that we have grown wiser in the last couple of days. We are now ready to move on. For the remainder of the week, we want to fix our eyes on Jesus. Just as stated in Hebrews 12:1-3, we desire to look directly to Him, not look away, to the left or right, but keep our focus on Him. He is the Author and Perfecter of our faith. He is the One we look to for direction—no one else will do. What an awesome testimony to us that we know we have Jesus as our perfect example, and He "has been tempted in all things as we are" (Hebrews 4:15). The difference is that He is without sin. Let's see how He faced all these temptations and still didn't sin.

Review Matthew 4:1-11 again to be reminded of the context of the situation. I believe there are three reasons Jesus was successful in warding off these temptations. May we be wise enough to follow in His footsteps.

1. **Jesus knew God's Word.**

Satan will do *anything* he can do to slip us up! Three times he tempted Jesus, and three times Jesus found power in God's spoken Word. What a blessing and lesson it is to us.

Read Isaiah 55:11 below and fill in the blanks.

"So will My _______________ be which goes forth from My mouth; It will not return to Me ________________, without accomplishing what I desire, and without succeeding in the matter for which I sent it."

This verse is such a comfort to me. Now read one more verse in Hebrews 4:12 about the power of God's Word. Then fill in the blanks below.

"For the word of God is __________________ and ________________ and

sharper than any two-edged sword, and piercing as far as the division of soul and spirit, of both joints and marrow, and able to ____________________ the thoughts and intentions of the heart."

God's Word is that powerful! It is amazing to think about. There is power in God's written Word, and just as powerful is the speaking of His Word. Jesus knew God's Word and used it to rid Himself of the enemy and to ward off his attacks. We are to do the same. We come to the point once again of asking ourselves the question:

If Jesus needed to know God's Word, how much more should I?

How do we come to know God's Word? We have to spend time in His Word and spend time meditating on and memorizing His Word. This is yet another aspect of abiding.

I want to point out one more important point before leaving this. Read verses 5-7 of Matthew 4 again. Did you notice that Satan knew God's Word as well? He knew it well enough to quote it to Jesus during the temptation. Though he used God's Word (Psalm 91:11-12) when speaking to Jesus, Satan twisted the context just enough to propose a test for Jesus. Jesus knew exactly what to do by not taking the challenge and instead returned the serve with one better—another Truth from God's Word. This exchange reminds me of Eve in the garden being tempted by the serpent. Satan took God's instructions to Eve and twisted them just enough to sound true, yet the statement was full of deceit (see Genesis 3:1-5). This should be a clear and strong warning for each of us about God's Word.

Read Psalm 119:11 and answer the following questions:

What do we need to hide or treasure in our hearts?

Why is it important?

We do need to hide or treasure God's Word in our hearts. By knowing God's Word, we are less likely to fall into temptation; we won't be fooled by the Deceiver. This brings us to our second point of Christ's success.

2. Jesus believed God's Word.

There is no doubt in my mind that Jesus not only knew God's Word, but believed it as well. I think we can all be guilty of not believing His Word without realizing it. We may know God's Word and even have many verses memorized, but we must believe God's Word as well. Yes, I know that sounds silly, and you are probably thinking, "Well, of course I believe it." However, when it comes down to trusting His Word and the power of His Word, I think many Christians, when tested, don't believe it. If we believed in His Word, then we would rely on it a lot more. We would look to His Word and the power of His Word for the answers to our every need. We would go to Him first rather than last. We would run, not walk, to Him when we are in a difficulty, an extended trial, or a temptation. Usually we rely on His Word last. Many times not at all. We go to counselors, pastors, teachers, friends—whomever we think has a better knowledge or connection with God.

Do you believe God's Word?

Do you run to His Word for healing, answers, and strength?

Where are you tempted to go instead?

Oh, dear friend, I am not trying to make you feel guilty, for I am guilty of this as well. I am trying to open our eyes—yours and mine—to the power that lies waiting for us. For when our eyes are opened, then we will get serious about treasuring God's Word in our hearts (see Ps. 119:11). Think about the awesome power we have been given through God's Word. Praise Him for it now!

Now we will look at our third and final reason for Jesus Christ's successful response to Satan.

3. Jesus kept an eternal focus.

I believe with all my heart that Jesus drew strength from keeping an eternal focus. Jesus knew when all was said and done that no matter what He endured there would be eternal benefits. Oh, how I pray that I continue to gain this perspective every single day. God has made me so very aware of the difference it makes when we live our lives in this manner, when we view our circumstances and trials with an eternal focus rather than a temporal one. Read the two verses below to understand what I mean.

"Behold, You have made my days as handbreadths, And my lifetime as nothing in Your sight; Surely every man at his best is a mere breath." (Psalm 39:5)

"Man is like a mere breath; His days are like a passing shadow." (Psalm 144:4)

According to the verses above, what is man at his best?

What are our days like?

You see, God is not saying that we aren't important. He created us and loves us unconditionally! However, we must learn from Jesus. First we must realize that this life truly is a temporary life. Compared to eternity, this is a brief visit! Second, Jesus could be all that He was and is for us because He knew what it would produce.

Read Hebrews 12:2 below.

"Fixing our eyes on Jesus, the author and perfecter of faith, who for the joy set before Him endured the cross, despising the shame, and has sat down at the right hand of the throne of God."

According to the verse, why did Jesus endure the cross?

What do you think the joy was?

After Jesus endured the cross, He sat at the right hand of God. God, His Father, sent Him to the cross so that He could be the Savior for our sins. God and Jesus had a purpose for the cross. This purpose was for you and me. He endured the cross for the joy that was set before Him. Ultimately you and I are the joy that was set before Him. He knew what enduring the cross would produce: The cross produced us a Savior who loves us so much He would do anything to spare us eternal damnation. Praise God! He went to the cross for you and for me. Have you thanked Him lately for it? If not, write your prayer of thankfulness to the Father for sending His Son, and then a prayer to the Son, Jesus, for enduring the cross because we are His joy, His delight!____

____

____

____

____

You may think that it was easy for Jesus because He had the benefit of knowing the future result. Well, believe it or not, we do as well. We may not be able to see the entire big picture, but we have the benefit of knowing God's Word and believing God's Word just as Jesus did! God tells us in His Word (Romans 8:28-29) His plan and His purpose for our lives. Let's repeat it once again: to be conformed into the image of His Son. We don't always know what the future holds for us, however, we do know who holds the future in His hands!

Let's close today's lesson by taking a personal inventory.

Do you know God's Word well enough to use it when you are tempted?

If not, what will you do to change that? Write your commitment now.

Has God shown you ways in which you haven't fully believed and relied on the power of His Word?

If so, write your prayer of confession and ask Him to give you the faith that you lack.

Lastly, do you have an eternal focus concerning this world?

If not, ask God to show you what you hold on to that keeps you from looking heavenward, and write it down.

Now commit all these things to Him, asking Him to bring honor and glory to Himself through you. God will reward your pure heart!

DAY 4: *We Are Not Alone*

Thank goodness, or I should say thank God, for the fact that He didn't leave us alone to try to make sense out of this world or to try to survive in this world on our own. I used to think how wonderful it would have been to live in the day of the apostles. To be able to walk with Him, talk with Him, and serve alongside Him was the most wonderful thing that I could imagine. Then I realized that in my naivety, I had failed to see how much better I have it than the apostles who walked along with Him. They were around Him only when He was physically with them. Since I am a child of God, I have Him with me all the time. He lives not only with me, but within me. The thought brings tears to my eyes. How blessed we are! When God took His Son home to heaven to return to His right hand, He didn't desert us. He left us with a Helper. Look up the following verses, noting what each one teaches us about our Helper, His role, who He is, and what He does.

John 14:16-17

John 14:25-26

John 16:7

Your notes probably include the following points: Our Helper is the Holy Spirit. He is with us forever, and He is the Spirit of Truth. He abides with us and within us. The Father sends the Holy Spirit to teach us and remind us of all that He has said. If Jesus would have remained with us, we would not have the Holy Spirit.

It is very important for us to know the role of the Holy Spirit so that we can be more attuned to His work in our lives. He does work in our lives every single day. Our job is to stay "tuned in," if you will, to what He is doing or trying to do in our lives. I refer to this concept as "flesh vs. Spirit." It refers to the war that is waging within us. We will study more of this tomorrow. Right now I want to share with you the three ways that we can hinder the Spirit in the work He is trying to accomplish within us. He is our Helper. We are to listen to Him, rely on Him, and obey Him when prompted by Him. Please realize that to understand this concept you first have to understand how important prayer and obedience is to our spiritual growth. Many times the Holy Spirit prompts us to do something, and at that moment we are faced with a choice. Our options are choosing to listen and obey or doing one of the following:

1. Quenching the Holy Spirit

1 Thessalonians 5:19 states, "Do not quench the Spirit." The word *quench* means "to

extinguish like fire, to suppress, to stifle." We have the ability to quench the Holy Spirit within us. The definition makes a very interesting point here, because when the Holy Spirit was first given, it came like tongues of fire (see Acts 2:3-4). So, to quench the Spirit is to extinguish or to suppress the flame. Let me try to give a personal example of this. Several years ago when I was studying and preparing a lesson on the Holy Spirit, I prayed and asked the Lord what "to quench" meant. At this same time I was going through a relationship healing time with a family member. Through a very hurtful family situation, many members of our family were hurt and many relationships damaged. I had once been very close to this particular person. Though my love for this person had not changed, the relationship had. We both (I believe) were working very hard to mend the relationship, and I desperately wanted it to be the same as before. I longed to be able to share openly as I once had. However, trust had been broken, and though both of us had forgiven one another, it just wasn't the same. I felt as though I had worked through the steps to forgiveness, however, each time we talked on the phone, things were not the same. I prayed to the Lord about this one day and asked Him to reveal to me what the matter was. I was sharing with Him how I truly believed I had forgiven her, but if I had, then why did I feel so different when I saw her or talked to her. At that very moment the Lord reminded me of this verse. "Do not quench the Spirit." I immediately had answers to both of my questions: What did "to quench" really mean, and why weren't things normal between us? I was quenching the Spirit. You see, when I thought of this person, I wasn't angry. Although the pain was still fresh, I had truly forgiven. However, when I heard this person's voice, I would let a wall go up in my spirit. This was a protection for myself to keep me from being hurt. The pain was so fresh and it had been so intense when the trust was lost that I was protecting myself from being hurt again, therefore, I would only let so much of me be vulnerable. It had nothing to do with forgiving. I was keeping the Holy Spirit from loving this person through me. In other words, instead of allowing what came to my mind to be expressed, I was building a wall of protection for my own sake. I was not allowing the Holy Spirit's love to flow through me in words and affection so that I wouldn't be hurt. I was quenching the Spirit. This revelation brought me to my knees where I quickly asked God's forgiveness. To know this accomplished several things in my life. I am now more aware of when I am about to quench the Spirit; I am now more sensitive to the Holy Spirit's prompting in this area, and I recognize how it has helped me in other difficult relationships as well.

I longed to be able to share openly as I once had. However, trust had been broken, and though both of us had forgiven one another, it just wasn't the same.

Has God brought a relationship to your mind in which you have quenched the Spirit when you are or were around this person?

If so, who is it, and what will you do about it?

I ask you right now to go to your knees with this relationship and ask God to make you keenly aware of your tendency to quench the love that God desires to lavish on this person through you.

2. Grieving the Holy Spirit

Ephesians 4:30 says, "Do not grieve the Holy Spirit of God, by whom you were sealed for the day of redemption." To grieve the Holy Spirit of God means "to make sorrowful, to cause distress." I believe we grieve the Holy Spirit when we are aware either of something that we know we should do and we refuse to do it, or something we should not do and we do it anyway. One example might be when I am faced with a choice to watch a movie that would bring dishonor to the Lord and I choose to watch it—let's say a movie that contains explicit sexual content or language that brings dishonor to the Lord and His name. Since the Holy Spirit is within me and He sees and hears what I see and hear, this would grieve Him. He is holy and trying to produce holiness in my life. He cannot do this while I am exposing myself to such evil.

Read 1 Corinthians 6:19-20 below.

"Or do you not know that your body is a temple of the Holy Spirit who is in you, whom you have from God, and that you are not your own? For you have been bought with a price: therefore glorify God in your body."

Exposure to evil will grieve the Holy Spirit every time, as will disobedience. This is just one small example of how we can grieve the Spirit of God. I am sure that I do it many times without knowing that I am grieving Him. That is why it is so important to be very alert to His work in our lives.

3. Lying to the Holy Spirit

The word *lie* means just what you would think, "to speak deliberate falsehoods."

Read Acts 5:1-11 to get the full story of two people who lied to the Holy Spirit. This is one you don't want to miss!

Ananias and his wife, Sapphira, are examples that we certainly don't want to follow in any way! They lied to the Holy Spirit and immediately fell down, dead. Notice verse 11—"and great fear came over the whole church, and over all who heard of these things." Can you imagine the moment? I don't blame that church one bit. I would have been scared out of my mind too! Now that we have heard about a true event involving a lie and the consequences of it, I think we will all be a little more careful with our tongues and our intentions before God.

We have now learned about our role in our relationship with the Holy Spirit and the three ways that we can hinder the Spirit's work in our lives. Don't ever forget that one of His names is Helper. He is within us to help us become more like the Son. I hope you can now see why the foundation of prayer was so important when we began this study. To have a lesson on obedience after studying about prayer really makes us think about the choices we make each day. Now we can fully understand the role we play in relation to the Holy Spirit and His promptings. Stop right now and ask the Lord to make you very sensitive to the Holy Spirit and your response to His every prompting. Then take a rest before we delve into tomorrow's lesson on the war that rages within.

DAY 5: *Flesh vs. Spirit*

I told you yesterday that we would dig into the roles of the flesh and the Spirit, and the war that rages within each of us. Please pray before you begin, asking the Lord to make known to you this struggle that we face daily. We will begin our reading in Romans.

Please read Romans 7:15, 19-20, 23-25 before going on.

Do you ever feel like Paul did when he spoke these words that you just read? I do! Read some of them again.

"For what I am doing, I do not understand; for I am not practicing what I would like to do, but I am doing the very thing I hate. . . . For the good that I want, I do not do, but I practice the very evil that I do not want. . . . Wretched man that I am! Who will set me free from the body of this death?" Romans 7:15, 19, 24

Sometimes I do the very thing I never intended or wanted to do, and sometimes I act in a way that I never intended to act. It is at these times that I, like Paul, want to scream, "Wretched woman that I am! Who will set me free from the body of this death?"

Why do we have this struggle? Read Galatians 5:17 below for your answer.

"For the flesh sets its desire against the Spirit, and the Spirit against the flesh; for these are in opposition to one another, so that you may not do the things that you please."

According to this verse, what two things are in opposition?

Just to clarify and make sure there is no confusion during our discussion today when we talk about the flesh and the Spirit, they will be defined as follows:

Spirit = Holy Spirit

Flesh (Greek word, *sarx*) = It means the flesh, denotes mere human nature, the earthly nature of man apart from divine influence and therefore prone to sin and opposed to God.

Our daily struggle and goal is to starve our flesh (our sinful nature) and feed the Spirit (the Holy Spirit within us). How exactly do we do that? Read Galatians 5:16-25 to find our answer. We will look at several of the verses in this passage to dig out the treasure in each. After you have read these verses, look again at verse 16:

"But I say, walk by the Spirit, and you will not carry out the desire of the flesh."

According to this verse, what are we to do?

This word translated *walk* literally means "to keep on walking, to be occupied." We are to occupy ourselves with the Spirit. To occupy myself I would need to be in His Word daily and remaining in a "spirit of prayer" as we have talked about. If I am focused on Him, then I won't be focused on self (flesh) and what my desires are. The best way to explain this would be to share with you something a friend said to me once. She was explaining how much she enjoyed listening to recordings of Christian speakers. She said she listens to them all the time and really likes to listen to them while on her treadmill. Her reasoning was that if she wasn't listening to Christian music or the teachings of God's Word, then her mind would wander and she would have to take her thoughts captive quite often. And she ended with, "And that's no fun!" This is so true. Our minds can be runaway trains. One wrong thought for some of us and we can work ourselves into a sinful fit. Stop your thoughts before they go too far. Walk by the Spirit and this isn't a problem.

Now look at verse 18.

"But if you are led by the Spirit, you are not under the Law."

What does this verse say our relationship with the Spirit should be?

To be led by the Spirit is to allow Him to lead, rule, and govern us. I believe this is an act of submission. We need to ask the Lord every day to show us through the Spirit what to do. We need to submit to His will and tell Him that we want to be that empty vessel, willing to be filled by Him and directed by Him.

The next verse in this passage to look at is verse 25:

"If we* live *by the Spirit, let us also* walk *by the Spirit." (emphasis mine)

Living by the Spirit means to be alive, under His constant guidance and influence. How do we do that? We must talk to Him in prayer all day, reminding ourselves that it is He who is in charge and not our flesh. The Word says that if we live by the Spirit, then we must also walk by the Spirit. This word for *walk* means "to walk by rule (orderly), to march in rank (military), step by step, like learning to walk." In other words, we should lean on Him for every step, decision, and move we make. We must learn to discern His will from our own. This implies a dependence upon Him for guidance and direction every step of the way. If I am living under His constant guidance and influence, then He will give my marching orders, I will conform to His ways, and I will follow Him step by step. I will be seeing less of my flesh and more of Him, and so will others! Filling my life with Him results in me *not* fulfilling the desires of the flesh.

Now let's go back to verse 24.

"Now those who belong to Christ Jesus have crucified the flesh with its passions and desires."

According to this verse, what has happened to the flesh?

Who has crucified the flesh?

This is a very important truth that we can't let slip by. "Crucified" is the Greek word *stauroo*, which means "to crucify the flesh along with its affections and lusts so as to mortify them through the faith and love of the crucified Christ."

If we have crucified the flesh, then why do you think we have such a struggle with it?

I believe there are a couple of reasons for this struggle. We have an enemy who entices us and tempts us to sin continuously. We also have our natural human nature which is bent toward sinning. The difference now is that before we came to know Jesus, we were slaves to sin, and now we are not. It may feel like we remain enslaved when we keep repeating the same sins over and over, however, we have been set free. In Galatians 5:1 we are told that it was for freedom we have been set free and are instructed to keep standing firm and not to be subjected again to a yoke of slavery. You know that we can sometimes be our own worst enemy. We can put ourselves into slavery through legalism or destructive behaviors which become habits, and then those habits become strongholds in our lives. The result is slavery. While reading verse 24, you cannot forget the verse that comes right after it which states, "If we live by the Spirit, let us also walk by the Spirit." Remember that living and walking by the Spirit is being under His constant guidance and influence and following Him step by step. We must follow Him constantly and obey His direction. When we obey the Holy Spirit we are crucifying the flesh—starving it!

Return to Galatians 5, read verses 19-23, and fill in the chart below.

Deeds of the flesh	**Fruit of the Spirit**

When we compare the deeds of the flesh to the fruit of the Spirit, it can seem overwhelming to see all we can struggle against. However, we can live our lives in such a way that we allow the fruit of the Spirit to shine through us. Turn to Romans 12:1-2 and read the verses. This is our answer to producing the fruits of the Spirit. We are not to conform to this world but to be "transformed by the ______________ ____ _____ ________________."

What does it mean to renew our minds? Renewing means to be qualitatively new, a renovation that makes a person different than in the past. There are four things that each of us can do to renew our minds constantly. This is a continual action; it is not something we do once and then we are finished.

1. Make God your priority in life.

Abide with God. He must come first before other things. As you spend time with Him each day, ask Him, "What are Your plans for me today; what do You want me to do today?" Whatever He tells you to do—obey Him!

2. Surround yourself with Him.

Listen to His Word being taught on Christian radio, podcasts, and CDs. Worship Him all day through Christian praise and worship music. Talk with Him all day as well. Don't treat Him as though He is at the place where you spent your time with Him last. He is with you always, no matter where you go.

3. Separate yourself from the things of the world.

Do this through times of fasting, silence and solitude, and separation from the massive amounts of communication we have. Be faithful to take time now and then as He leads to turn off the phone, TV, computer, or other devices and just focus on Him with praise music or no music. Spend time listening to Him in silence. Sometimes this separation is simply making pure and good choices about what we allow into our minds. We have to be careful about what we read, listen to, look at, and watch. If we are not careful, we can easily become desensitized to the harshness of this world. Through humor and other avenues, the world finds ways for sin to not seem so evil. We must be very careful about what we allow into our minds, so that when evil comes our way it is a shock to us.

4. Practice the spiritual disciplines.

Donald Whitney said in his book, *Spiritual Disciplines for the Christian Life*, "The spiritual disciplines are those personal and corporate disciplines that promote spiritual growth."[8] There are more than I can list, but in addition to the ones Bible study and prayer, some other disciplines are: service, stewardship, confession, worship, fasting, solitude, learning, and evangelism. By practicing the disciplines, we are pursuing godliness. God's Word tells us to discipline ourselves for the purpose of godliness (see 1 Timothy 4:7). Two books I would recommend on this subject are *Spiritual Disciplines for the Christian Life* by Donald Whitney and *The Life You've Always Wanted* by John Ortberg.

All the above are keys to renewing our minds. I truly could spend days on this lesson. However, my hope and prayer is that you are more aware of this battle that rages within us and all around us. We have already won the war. Christ defeated Satan when He died and rose again. However, I want to live victoriously as a Christian and not just survive. How about you? Remember, it was for freedom that Christ set us free (see Galatians 5:1). I am praying for you!

Week 4

Jesus: His Example of Loving Others

"And walk in love, just as Christ also loved you and gave Himself up for us, an offering and a sacrifice to God as a fragrant aroma." Ephesians 5:2

Day 1
God Is Love

Day 2
He Loves Us!

Day 3
Love in Action

Day 4
Serving Up Love

Day 5
How Am I Loving?

Memory and Meditation: "This is My commandment, that you love one another, just as I have loved you." John 15:12

Prayer: *Dear heavenly Father, we come to You asking that You do a mighty work in our hearts this week. Lord, teach us to love as You love. Teach us what unconditional love looks like, acts like, and feels like. You are love, dear Lord, and we are able to love because You first loved us. Show us how Jesus demonstrated such a love for others even in the midst of betrayal, suffering, and pain. Lord, we want to learn from the example of Your Son. Teach us this kind of love so that we may learn to walk in love every day. Lord, may we learn so much about Your love that we draw others to You because of the love that flows out of our lives. Father, give us a tender heart and spiritual eyes and ears so that we are sensitive to Your Spirit.* **Amen.**

Week 4

Jesus: His Example of Loving Others

"And walk in love, just as Christ also loved you and gave Himself up for us, an offering and a sacrifice to God as a fragrant aroma." Ephesians 5:2

Day 1: *God Is Love*

We have studied Christ's example regarding prayer, obedience, and facing temptation. Now we will move to His wonderful example of love. I can hardly wait for you to see how He demonstrated for us examples of love everywhere we look in Scripture. We can so easily overlook them and never pick out the treasure hidden between the lines of the stories told. Pray right now that this week you don't miss a single bit. This week's lesson is a precious testimony of Christ's example of loving others, yet it can be hard when we face the personal application. To get to this point of following Christ requires a life of prayer, a life of obedience, and an understanding of how to deal with the temptations that we face. This lesson could change your life. Not only that, but it could change the lives of all those around you! I am praying for you!

Let's get started by first taking a look at what God's Word says about love. Read the entire passage, and then we will delve deeper into the verses one by one.

Read 1 John 4:7-21.

Focus on verses 7 and 8 to answer the following questions.

Where does love come from?

If we do not love, what does it say about us?

Finish the statement: (vs. 8) "For God is ________________."

Verses 9 and 10:

God sent His only Son into the world so that we might what? (vs. 9)

What did God do for us? (vs. 10)

Why?

Verses 11 and 12:

Since God loves us, what should we do?

If we love one another, what does God do?

And His love is what?

Verses 13 and 14:

What has He given us?

Again, what has the Father sent the Son to do?

Verses 15 and 16:

If we confess that Jesus is the Son of God, what happens?

God is what?

What is the result for one who abides in love?

Verses 17 and 18:

As a result of the above, what happens?

Why?

What does perfect love cast out?

Verses 19-21:

Why do we love?

If we do not love our brother who we have seen, then what does Scripture say about our love for God?

If we love God, then who are we capable of loving?

Whose commandment is this?

From this passage we learn several things about love. I will list them below in the order they appeared in Scripture. From 1 John 4:7-21 we learned:

- We are to love one another.
- Love is from God.
- Everyone who loves is born of God.

- Everyone who loves knows God.
- The one who does not love does not know God.
- God is love.
- God loves us.
- We are to love one another.
- If we love one another, God abides in us and His love is perfected in us.
- God is love.
- The one who abides in love abides in God.
- God abides in the one who abides in love.
- If God abides in us, love is perfected with us.
- There is no fear in love.
- Perfect love casts out fear.
- The one who fears is not perfected in love.
- We love because God first loved us.
- If we love God, then we cannot hate our brother.
- If we love God, we love our brother also.
- To love our brother is a commandment from God.

I'm sure you noticed that some of the truths about love were repeated in Scripture. I think this is because God wanted to emphasize these truths. Go back through the above list and put a star next to or highlight the three that spoke most powerfully to you.

Now rewrite those three on the lines below, making them personal by adding to the sentence or by inserting your name in the sentence. (See the example below.)

1. If God abides in Lori, love is perfected in Lori.
2. Lori loves because God first loved Lori.
3. Lori is to love others as God loves Lori.

After spending a lot of time praying about this lesson, I don't think there is one thing that God desires for me to add. This is what I ask you to do: Stop what you are doing and pray right now. Ask God to help you to understand His love, and ask Him to speak to you through His Word. Now go back and read through your answers as you reread the Scripture. Sit quietly before Him and allow your mind to absorb all that this passage says about His love for us and our love for Him and others. Make notes as you go on this page or in your Bible. Close today's lesson by writing your prayer to Him about love. Don't skip this. I believe God has a special message for you today. Sit and listen to Him now.

Day 2: *He Loves Us!*

Today we want to learn exactly what "to love" means. God does love us, but what exactly does that mean? That is what we will study today: God's love. I want to share with you that this has been the most challenging lesson to write thus far. The reason for this is because it is so difficult to explain and to comprehend His love. I cannot fathom God's love. I believe it is beyond what I can imagine. His love knows no bounds and is completely unselfish. Why is that hard for me to understand? Because it doesn't come naturally for me. I am praying now even as I write that I can do justice in explaining God's undeniable love for you and me.

Let's first start by looking into this word *love* and its meaning. The passage of Scripture that you looked at yesterday is filled with the word love. Every use of this word in 1 John 4:7-21 is derived from the same word for love. The passage uses the two Greek words *agapao* and *agape*. One is a noun, and one is a verb. After studying for hours trying to find a good working definition for you, I found that I couldn't. It was then that God brought me to Ephesians 3:19, which states, "And to know the love of Christ which surpasses knowledge, that you may be filled up to all the fullness of God." I hope you saw what I saw when I read this Scripture. If you didn't see it, then read the first part of the verse again. No wonder I kept racking my brain and still could not explain God's love. *It surpasses knowledge!* God's love surpasses our understanding. That is why I couldn't bring myself to describe it, nor could I find an adequate definition by theologians to explain it.

The best definition I found is the following: "In respect of *agapao* as used of God, it expresses the deep and constant 'love' and interest of a perfect Being toward entirely unworthy objects, producing and fostering a reverential 'love' in them toward the Giver, and a practical 'love' toward those who are partakers of the same, and a desire to help others to seek the Giver."[9] Even this definition misses being complete. The best I can say is that God's love is expressed through His actions. The following is a list of actions (just a few) that I believe demonstrate His love better than we can explain His love:

- God sent His Son, Jesus, to be our Savior by dying on the cross for *our* sins (John 3:16).
- God is faithful and just to forgive us for our sins (1 John 1:9).
- God will never leave us nor forsake us (Heb. 13:5).
- God has a plan for our lives—a plan that is good (Jer. 29:11).
- God will work all things together for good to those who love Him (Rom. 8:28).
- God is conforming us into the image of His Son (Rom. 8:29).

How has God demonstrated His love for you? List a few of your own ideas by the bullets below. Use Scripture—if possible—to support what He promised He would do.

-
-
-
-

The bottom line is that God loves us. He loves us with a pure, undefiled, and unselfish love. We cannot love like that without first loving Him. And the only reason we can love Him is because He first loved us. The only way we can love in this pure, unselfish, and undefiled manner is by allowing Him to fill us up with His love so that it overflows to others. How? When we accept Christ as our Lord and Savior, the Holy Spirit comes to dwell within us. Because we have God living within us, we can allow God to love others through us. One of the joys of the Christian life is witnessing God develop this fruit of love within ourselves and within others. God is always true to His Word. As you remember, John 15:5 states, "I am the vine, you are the branches; he who abides in Me and I in him, he bears much fruit, for apart from Me you can do nothing."

According to this verse, can we love others if we are not abiding?

Read John 15:8.

How is the Father glorified?

If we bear fruit, what will it prove?

Taking into account all that you have studied yesterday and today, what is one fruit that we will bear if we are abiding?

Read Galatians 5:22-23 to find out what type of fruits are borne through the Holy Spirit within us. List below all the fruits of the Spirit named.

-
-
-
-
-
-
-
-
-

What is the first fruit of the Spirit listed?

Read 1 Corinthians 13:1-13 to learn more about love; then complete the following:

Reread verses 1-3 and summarize in your own words what these verses mean to you.

List below what love is and what love is not according to verses 4-8.

Love is/does	**Love is not/does not**

Which is the greatest attribute of the three listed in verse 13?

No matter what we do, we cannot get away from the truth of Scripture about love. If we are abiding, then we will be loving others. We will love unselfishly with a love that draws others to Him. The love of God is what this world needs to see more of, isn't it? It starts with us. Go back to 1 Corinthians 13:4-8 in your Bible. Read what love is, but replace the word *love* with your name. As you do this, think about the people you are closest to. It may be your spouse or your children. As you read through these verses, think about whether you can say that you demonstrate this kind of love to them. For example, "Lori is patient, Lori is kind . . ." See how far you get before you feel convicted. Write what the Lord says to you about this exercise below.

Now close in prayer, asking God to work in your life in such a way to bring about this fruit so that you may prove to be His disciple and He will be glorified through you (see John 15:8). May God bless your heart for Him!

Day 3: *Love in Action*

I am not sure if I can think of a time when the Holy Spirit's impression upon me was so strong, and came from out of nowhere, as when I was prompted with what we will study today. The prompting came from me asking a simple question: "How am I to love?" I had entreated the Lord over and over again, needing to know how to handle a very painful situation that I was in. It was a situation that had happened before, just with different circumstances. I can say very frankly that I have had to learn to love like God does through years of hurtful, painful, personal experiences, and years of entreating the Lord to teach me what His love looks like.

I grew up in a home without much physical or verbal affection. Our affection was expressed through teasing. If you came to my house and my family liked you, you would know by the way they joked and teased with you. This has been an area where the Lord has had to work in my life, laying bits and pieces throughout my life to show me what His love looks like. I wanted my children to "know that they know" that no matter what, they are loved. All of us need to know that, don't we? I tell them I love them constantly. Even when we have disagreements, I make sure to tell them that I love them.

I had been struggling for some time with how to handle a repeat situation with people I deeply care about. The circumstances were different, but overall the situation was the same: Christians cutting other Christians out of their lives. This time the circumstances held higher stakes than the first time around. The hurt was that much deeper because it involved my children, and it opened a wound that had never fully healed from the previous severing of relationship ties. I had replayed the old script in my mind over and over again. "How do I love them, Lord?" was the question to which I desperately needed the answer. What I was really asking was, "What will it look like?" I already knew there was no question that I must love, but what it was to look like in action with these circumstances was the more poignant question I was asking.

One particular morning we, as a family, were on our way to church. We were listening to praise music, and I wasn't even thinking of our current situation, when a question from the Lord was impressed in my spirit. The question was, "Why did my Son heal the man's ear?" I immediately knew that the Lord was asking me this to answer my question about loving others. I could not remember the story or ever hearing anyone teach on it, so I asked Steve, "Did Jesus heal the man's ear?" After discussing it for a couple of minutes, we decided that He did, but we weren't sure of the circumstances surrounding the incident. At that moment I could hardly wait to get home to study this story, for I knew this was the Lord's answer to my cry, "How am I to love?"

Do you have someone in your life who is difficult to love?

It may be only one person or it could be many. Please stop for one moment and prayerfully think about this. You may have already forgiven them, but still find it difficult to love them. Look at the list below and write the names or initials of people or a person under each heading.

Easy to Love	Difficult to Love	Don't Want to Love

Now let's turn to Jesus and His example so that we can learn how we are to love. We have four different accounts of this one event. We will first start in Matthew as we move through three of the accounts, gleaning what details we can from each of the three.

First, let me share with you the context of this passage in Matthew 26. During our week of study on obedience, we read all around this passage, but stopped just before this account. Jesus and His disciples were in the Garden of Gethsemane, and Jesus has just finished praying. In previous verses in this chapter, Jesus had stated that "the hour is at hand" (vs. 45) and "the one who betrays Me is at hand" (vs. 46). We will look more in depth at this later. For now let's focus on Matthew 26:48-52, then answer the questions.

Who was struck with a sword? (vs. 51)

What happened to him?

Do we know (at this point) who struck him?

Who put a stop to the violence?

Now read John 18:10-11 to find more detail.

Who was the one who used the sword?

What was the (high priest's) slave's name?

Once again, who put a stop to the violence?

Though Mark gives another narrative, we are going straight to Luke for our final reading on this subject. Turn to Luke 22:49-54 and read it. From all the Scripture put together, we know that Peter is the one who drew the sword and struck the high priest's slave, whose name was Malchus. Please answer the following questions.

Why do you think Peter did this?

Who stopped him from doing more?

What did Jesus do after he told Peter to put away the sword? (vs. 51)

I find it so very interesting that of all four accounts, only Luke shares that Jesus reached over and healed Malchus's ear. Luke, who by trade was a physician, shares how the Great Physician healed this slave's ear. What a beautiful picture this is of Jesus' love. The question that the Holy Spirit prompted me to ask of this situation is simply, "Why?" Why do you think Jesus healed this slave's ear?" List all the possible reasons you can think of before going on. ________

____

____

____

____

Since I pondered this quite a bit after studying it and in the years since, let me share with you some questions I asked myself as to why Jesus might have done this.

- Did Jesus think this man would have a change of heart?
- Would seeing Christ heal him change this man?
- Would this man suddenly believe in Jesus' power and believe that He was who He said He was?
- Would he suddenly believe in Jesus as the Son of God, the Savior of his sins, and not arrest Him?
- Or—was Jesus doing it for the sake of the others around who were watching?
- Would they believe in Him and in God when they witnessed Jesus' ability and power to heal?

I have read all around this passage trying to find one of the above purposes for Jesus healing Malchus. I fully believe that God has multiple purposes in all that He does, and we can't even begin to understand, fathom, or "get" all of them. However, considering how God spoke so clearly to me that particular morning, assuring me this was indeed the answer for which I was looking, I am convinced that the answer lies in the example of Christ. Let me share with you what I believe the Lord wanted me to learn from this great act of mercy and compassion.

Remember, in response to my question, "How am I to love?" the Lord answered with a question to me, "Why did My Son heal the man's ear?" Jesus knew this act would not change circumstances; the man still took Him to the cross. So why did Jesus do this? It was an act of love. Don't move forward too fast without letting yourself absorb what I am saying. Let me repeat it again: This was an act of *agape* love. Jesus knew that this would not change His circumstances, however, He loved anyway. As far as we know, the man's heart didn't change; he didn't change what he came to do, and he didn't fall down to worship God's Son. Those around didn't do any of the above either. Jesus did it because this is what God's love demonstrated looks like. True *agape* love doesn't expect anything in return. Agape love reaches out to love when love isn't deserved or reciprocated, and does so without expectations.

What was God saying to me? He was telling me to love others the way His Son loved. His Son knew what would happen, yet He loved in the face of hate. That is how I am to love. I am to love others with a pure love no matter what they do to me. I love them because God loves them, and He wants them to experience His love through me.

Jesus healing the soldier's ear is Christ's love in action for us to see. When I asked the Lord how I was supposed to love these people who had hurt me so deeply again and again, this is where the Lord pointed me. I was to follow His Son. You see, these people were taking Jesus to the cross. They had come to arrest Him. And as He pointed out, He had been with them in the temple every day and they never laid a hand on Him, now they came with swords and clubs. Jesus was leaving His example all over the pages of Scripture because He knew that we needed a true and pure example to follow. He knew that He was going to the cross, and healing Malchus's ear would not change that. So why did He do it? So we could learn from His example of expressing love and compassion—no matter what the circumstances are that we face.

If you are like me, it is hard to love others, especially to love others who don't love us. But even harder still is to love when doing so doesn't change another's actions toward us. However, Jesus loved, knowing all of this. Why? God is love. The Father and Son are One, therefore, God's love was flowing through the Son.

**If Jesus loved all others, even those who did not love Him,
how much more should I?**

To love as God loves is a challenge, and one we are not capable of apart from the Holy Spirit within us. Read John 15:9-12.

What is the commandment that God gives us in verse 12?

According to these verses, what must we do to love in this way?

Do you love others as God has loved you?

Is your love based on what you will receive from others?

Look back over your list of people you wrote down. Are you willing to obey and love as Jesus did? It is usually pretty easy to love our spouse, children, or best friend. However, to love them with an *agape* love can be hard at times. But what about loving the list of "difficult to love" people? Will you love them with an *agape* love?

What about those names on your list of "people I don't want to love?" Will you love those with an agape love?

Remember that to love like this, we must be abiding. We also must make a choice to obey. Go to God with the request for Him to teach you how to love like Jesus loved. Go to your face, if necessary, in humility and reverence to your Lord like Jesus did and entreat the Lord. Tell Him you desire to please Him more than you desire to withhold His love from others. If you don't have the desire, ask Him to change your heart to give you the desire, because He will. He just needs a willing vessel that is willing to have a heart transplant!

Write your prayer to Him, listing every person whom you need a desire to love as Jesus has loved you. ____

____

____

____

____

If you have failed to love any of those people on your list, ask God's forgiveness. Now go to each of them as He leads and ask their forgiveness as well. This is hard, but if you are abiding He will give you the strength to obey! I am praying for you!

Day 4: *Serving Up Love*

I hope you were blessed by yesterday's lesson. God's love can truly transform us. I believe that when we have our eyes focused on Him and we are following Him, the natural progression is for so many of His attributes to flow out of our lives. However, we still have that battle of the flesh and Spirit going on inside us. My desire is not for us to beat ourselves up in all the ways we have failed to love. My desire is to get you into God's Word to understand what He says about the way we are to live and love. His Word is alive and active and sharper than any two-edged sword (see Hebrews 4:12). His Word does indeed change us. Praise Him for that!

Today we will study another example of Christ's amazing love. The event we will read about is the Last Supper. In the very first verse it says that Jesus knows that His hour has come.

Read John 13:1-15 slowly and prayerfully then answer the questions below so that we establish the context of the situation:

According to verse 2, what has happened to Judas Iscariot?

Did Jesus know who would betray Him? (If unsure, read verse 11.)

Who refused to have Jesus wash his feet? (vs. 8)

Why do you think he didn't want Jesus to wash his feet?

Would you have a hard time letting Jesus wash your feet?

Why?

Now read verses 36-38 of the same chapter.

What did Jesus tell Peter he would do?

Now read John 18:1-27, making notes below of what Judas did and what Peter did. As you make your notes, write down what verse you found your information in. Also note each time that Peter denied Christ and what verse it is in. ______________________________

To get a clearer picture of exactly what Judas did, read Matthew 26:46-50.

In verse 50 what did Jesus call Judas?

This is the Greek *hetairos*. It is a kindly address, meaning "my good friend." When Jesus was greeting Judas, He was not intending to voice sarcasm, to speak in anger, or to belittle him. He was sincere. Jesus knew Judas was there to betray Him and had already betrayed Him for money, yet He greeted him as His good friend.

Let's recap exactly what we know about Jesus, Peter, and Judas:

- Peter told Jesus he would lay down his life for Him (John 13:37-38).
- Jesus knew that Peter would deny Him three times.
- Peter was willing to fight for Jesus and defend Him with a sword, yet within hours denied knowing Jesus three times.
- Jesus knew Judas would betray Him.
- Judas betrayed Jesus for money.
- Judas led the Roman cohort to Christ in the garden.

Knowing all the above, what had Jesus done for Judas *and* Peter prior to partaking in the Lord's Supper? (Go back to John 13:1-15.)

Jesus tells them that since He washed their feet, they should do what (vs. 14)?

What did He tell them was the reason for washing their feet (vs. 15)? Write the verse out below. (This verse is the theme verse for our entire study.)_____________________________

____

____

____

I have said it before, but I must say it again. I am overwhelmed by Christ's love. He knew Judas would betray Him, yet He washed His feet lovingly. He knew Peter would deny Him three times even after saying he would die for Him, yet He washed Peter's feet lovingly. He greeted Judas as His good friend, knowing that Judas had brought the men who would take Him to the cross.

Have you ever loved someone in this manner?

Are you willing to try?

Are you willing to love all the people God places in your life in this way and to this extent?

If so, then write your prayer to the Lord now, making this a commitment before Him.

____

____

____

____

Read one last verse before we close today. Pay attention to the last few words in italics.

Now before the Feast of the Passover, Jesus knowing that His hour had come that He would depart out of this world to the Father, having loved His own who were in the world, **He loved them to the end.*" John 13:1*** (emphasis mine)

The NIV states, "He showed them the full extent of His love."

Meditate on this verse and then write back to the Lord your thoughts and what He has said to you today.

How many people will you be able to say this about: "I loved them to the end" or "I showed them 'the full extent of His love?"

Oh, heavenly Father, work in our hearts so that we may be tender to sharing Your love with others all around us. Father, someday we want to be able to say that we loved everyone you placed in our lives to the full extent of Your love. Amen.

Day 5: *How Am I Loving?*

Today we want to allow God to use all that we have read and studied to help us examine our own lives in light of His Word. We also will look at additional Scripture that will enable us to allow God's Word to illuminate areas that have been hidden from His counsel and His righteousness. We have ignored some of these areas because of ignorance. Some we have kept hidden because we didn't want to know Truth. Others are just areas of sin that we allowed to creep in so slowly through another door that we didn't realize they were there. No matter how they got there, I pray right now that you will allow God's transforming power to go to work in your life. I pray that you will "feed the Spirit" and "starve the flesh" until God is allowed to permeate your life with His transforming Word.

Let's start by getting our hearts readied and right before Him. Read Psalm 1:1-3 and Psalm 17:7-11. After reading all of these verses, write a prayer based on these Scriptures of what you would like God to do in your life today regarding His love. There is no right or wrong, this is between you and the Lord. Prepare your heart before Him. ______________________________

____

____

____

____

Now that you are prepared to hear from Him, read Luke 6:27-35 below and fill in the blanks following the passage.

> ***"But I say to you who hear, love your enemies, do good to those who hate you, bless those who curse you, pray for those who mistreat you. Whoever hits you on the cheek, offer him the other also; and whoever takes away your coat, do not withhold your shirt from him either. Give to everyone who asks of you, and whoever takes away what is yours, do not demand it back. Treat others the same way you want them to treat you. If you love those who love you, what credit is*** **that** ***to you? For even sinners love those who love them. If you do good to those who do good to you, what credit is*** **that** ***to you? For even sinners do the same. If you lend to those from whom you expect to receive, what credit is*** **that** ***to you? Even sinners lend to sinners in order to receive back the same*** **amount**. ***But love your enemies, and do good, and lend, expecting nothing in return; and your reward will be great, and you will be sons of the Most High; for He Himself is kind to ungrateful and evil men."***

Who are we to love?

Who are we to do good to?

Who are we to bless?

And who are we to pray for?

How are we to treat others?

This word for enemies refers to opponents. They could be believers or unbelievers. How are we to be different from them?

Again, who are we to love?

What type of love would this be?

What will happen to us as a result of loving this way?

Who is God Himself kind to?

Jesus is saying that even "sinners," or irreligious people, may have enough grace to forgive their opponents. We should be different from them—we should stand out from others in reference to the love that flows out of us.

Look up the following Scriptures and write what each says about love. Then record how well you think you have done regarding love based upon these verses.

Matthew 22:37-38

Romans 12:9-10

Romans 13:8, 10

1 John 3:10-11

1 Peter 4:8

Ephesians 5:2

Proverbs 10:12

Proverbs 17:17

1 Corinthians 16:14

I know this is not easy; to put ourselves under the microscope of God's Word is difficult. Yet this is what we need to do to allow God to change us and transform us into the image of His Son. When we put ourselves before the Lord and ask Him to show us the error of our ways, then we are seeking His righteousness. Look up Psalm 11:7 to see what God says about those who are righteous.

According to this verse what does the Lord love?

What does He say will happen to the upright?

So, what do we do about those who dislike us strongly or even hate us?

Yes, we love them with God's love: His *agape* love. We allow Him to love them through us. And what if they don't love us in return? We look to Jesus, the author and perfecter of faith (see Hebrews 12:2). We look to His example (see John 13:15) and we follow it.

HIS LOVE IS . . . washing the feet of the one He knew would betray Him.

HIS LOVE IS . . . washing the feet of the one who would soon deny knowing Him.

HIS LOVE IS . . . reaching over and healing the severed ear of the one who would deliver Him to the cross.

HIS LOVE IS . . . dying on the cross for the sake of others.

HIS LOVE IS . . . taking the punishment of billions and billions, knowing that many will never receive or accept His love.

HIS LOVE IS . . . loving all others to the end.

Thank Him now for His love, and ask Him to perfect it in you. And when it gets hard to love those who don't love you in return, meditate on the Psalm below.

"I love You, O Lord, my strength."
The Lord is my rock and my fortress and my deliverer,
My God, my rock, in whom I take refuge;

My shield and the horn of my salvation, my stronghold.
I call upon the LORD, who is worthy to be praised,
And I am saved from my enemies."
Psalm 18:1-3

Father, teach us to love as You love. Amen.

Week 5

Jesus: His Example of Forgiveness

"When you were dead in your transgressions and the uncircumcision of your flesh, He made you alive together with Him, having forgiven us all our transgressions." Colossians 2:13

Day 1
A Small Glimpse

Day 2
A Big Word

Day 3
An Exception

Day 4
Satan's Attempt

Day 5
God's Gift

Memory and Meditation Verse: "Be kind to one another, tender-hearted, forgiving each other, just as God in Christ also has forgiven you." Ephesians 4:32

Prayer: *Precious heavenly Father, we praise Your holy name. You indeed are the giver of all good and perfect gifts. We thank You, Father, for what You have taught us through the example of Your Son. We pray now that You will pierce our hearts with the truth of Your Word. Teach us about forgiveness, Father. Teach us to forgive as You forgive. Show us when we are unwilling to forgive and how our unwillingness to forgive can damage our relationship with You. Lord, reveal to us how, when we truly forgive, You use that to draw others to Yourself. Lord, I pray for transparency in all of us this week. I pray we open all areas in our lives so that You can completely clean them out. Lord, help us, comfort us, lead us, and direct us.* **Amen**.

Week 5

Jesus: His Example of Forgiveness

"When you were dead in your transgressions and the uncircumcision of your flesh, He made you alive together with Him, having forgiven us all our transgressions." Colossians 2:13

DAY 1: *A Small Glimpse*

I would guess that this week's lesson could be the hardest for many of us. The subject of forgiveness penetrates every area of our lives. It is also one that is a constant in our lives. There is always someone or something to forgive! If we are honest, we are also always in need of asking for forgiveness as well. The thing about it is that it won't get much better as long as our world continues to decline into the sea of sin. Some of us have a lot to forgive. Some of us probably have a lot to ask forgiveness for. Some of us need to forgive ourselves, but we just haven't realized it yet. The great news is that we have a perfect example. Jesus Christ, the Son of God, is the perfect example for us to follow regarding forgiveness! This week we will spend our time looking at His example, understanding what forgiveness is and discovering how we come to the place of forgiving. Hang tough this week. It may be hard for you, but the rewards of walking through this week with Him cannot even be explained. I am praying for you!

I liken dealing with issues of forgiveness to falling down and scraping our knees. I can remember my son falling down as a child and scraping both knees. I remember how we cleaned them, put medicine on them, and placed bandages on the wounds. I also remember well that after a week or so, one knee had healed and the other had not. We quickly realized that we had not cleaned the wound as carefully as we should have. As we looked closely, we saw that one knee had a little bump under the skin, which was keeping it from healing properly. We told our son that there was a small piece of gravel there and that we needed to open the wound to get it out so it could heal properly. Of course, he didn't want us coming close to him with a needle, and he certainly could not stand the thought of us digging around on his sore knee. We knew, though, that this was what had to be done. We also knew that it would be painful, but not as painful as leaving it there. That is what this week might be like for some of you. It might be painful. Although my son knew that it would be painful, we also convinced him it would be best to open it, get the tiny piece of gravel out, and put some medicine on it. So it is with forgiveness. Think of it as placing alcohol on a wound. It will sting a bit, but afterwards it will heal properly. You will be thankful that you endured the pain because of the results it brings. I am pleading with you to face the pain. Whatever comes up this week, face it with God. Let Him walk you through it; pour your heart out to Him, and face it with Him. There can be no one else better to face it with, and no one better to learn about forgiveness from, than Jesus Himself.

We will first look at the ultimate in forgiveness. Read Luke 23:1-26 to understand the full context leading up to the point of Jesus' death on the cross.

According to verse 2, what was the Sanhedrin accusing Jesus of?

When Jesus was asked the question, "Are you the King of the Jews?" what did Jesus answer?

Pilate said he could find no guilt in Jesus. So, in verse 5 what did the people accuse Jesus of?

In verse 10 what were the chief priests and the scribes doing while standing there?

They accused Jesus in a forceful and strong manner. Then according to verse 11, what did they do to Jesus?

Before we go any further, list all the ways in which Christ was mistreated *before* going to the cross. Matthew gives the most detail of Jesus' suffering, so we will first go there and then to John. The verses are listed below. Look them up and then list what they did to Jesus.

Matthew 27:26

Matthew 27:28

Matthew 27:29

Matthew 27:30

Matthew 27:31

Matthew 27:34

John 19:3

Let's go a step further to understand how much Jesus suffered. Matthew 27:26 and Mark 15:15 state that Jesus was "scourged" (NIV says "flogged"). This is the Greek word *phragelloo*. The following is the definition of scourging taken from Vine's Expository Dictionary: "Under the Roman method of 'scourging,' the person was stripped and tied in a bending posture to a pillar, or stretched on a frame. The 'scourge' was made of leather thongs, weighted with sharp pieces of bone or lead, which tore the flesh of both the back and the breast." It is almost unbearable to think about, isn't it? Read it again so you do not take lightly what Jesus endured for us. It is no wonder He didn't have the strength to carry the cross to Golgotha.

Now reread Luke 23:13-16.

Had Pilate or Herod found any guilt in Jesus?

In verse 16, what did Pilate say he was going to do?

Turn to Matthew 27:19 to find another reason Pilate wanted to release Jesus.

What had happened?

Based on Luke 23:18-25, who did the people want released instead of Jesus?

What had this man done?

It is almost unbelievable, isn't it? These people were in a frenzy. They would rather have had a murderer on the loose who was a rebel and revolutionary than to have Jesus on the loose.

What do you think was really behind all of this anger and hate?

Look at Mark 15:10-11 to find out who and what was driving these people to persecute Christ.

Jesus was suffering because of envy, plain and simple—the four-letter word that leads to great strife, distress, and hurt. I have seen envious people do some very bizarre and crazy things, as well as hurtful things. What about you? Have you ever been persecuted because of someone's envy?

More importantly, have you ever done wrong to another because you were envious of them? Let God answer this one for you; sit and wait right now for His answer to this question. Write below what He has said to you. ____
____
____
____
____
____

Now write what God would have you do about what He has revealed to you. If you have done wrong to others, take it to your heavenly Father, and ask for His forgiveness. Then go to the person and ask his or her forgiveness as well. ______________________________________
____
____
____
____

Asking for another's forgiveness is hard, but we must desire to obey God more than man or our flesh! If you find that this will be very hard for you, give yourself a deadline to get it done, and pray every day for God's wisdom, perfect timing, and courage for you to do exactly what He desires for you to do.

Envy and hurtful actions from others are painful, no matter their cause, but they are especially painful when they are unjustified.

Why do you think the chief priests were so envious of Christ?

Look up Mark 7:20-23 and write what Jesus said about envy.

We need to be very aware of envy that springs up from within us. Ask the Lord to make you aware of any and all envy in your life, and to draw your attention to the sin immediately so that you can take it captive before it defiles you. I would proclaim Jesus an expert on the dramatic effects of envy and what could happen as a result of it.

Now return to Luke 23:22-26.

Pilate wanted to release Jesus, so in verse 22, what does he tell the crowd he will do?

In verses 23-25, what finally happens?

Here we see Pilate give in to the demands of the people. Pilate, who wanted nothing more than to release Jesus, gave in to the pressure. Pilate, who had washed his hands in front of the people and claimed that he would not be responsible for this man's blood, just gave up (see Matthew 27:24)! I cannot help but think about all the regrets these people had once they realized whom they had crucified. Think about a time in your life when you thought you were so right about something and then later found out how wrong you were. Now relate that to their feelings. Except here we are talking about more than a minor mistake; we are talking about these men realizing that they had just sentenced the Savior of the world to die on the cross. We are talking about *their very own* Savior—they helped send Him to the cross. Thank God that He is as His name states, our Savior! We all need one. There is nothing we have done that He cannot forgive. It is His very nature to forgive.

Is there something in your life that you have never brought before the Lord because you were too ashamed or thought that He could not or would not forgive you? What is it?

Take it to Him now and ask His forgiveness. He is the King of forgiveness. He is ready to hear you and grant you His forgiveness. Praise Him for that right now by writing your prayer of thankfulness below for His willingness to go to the cross on our behalf, even in the midst of horrific circumstances. Remember that we are the ones who deserved to be where Jesus was!

Thank You, Father, for Your amazing love for us expressed in the suffering of Your Son. Amen!

DAY 2: *A Big Word*

Yesterday we began our journey into Jesus' walk toward the cross. Today we will continue that journey to get the bigger picture of exactly what Jesus Christ endured on our behalf. Pray now for God to make you very aware of His loving presence and His willingness to forgive no matter what the circumstances.

Yesterday we stopped just as the decision had been made to release Barabbas instead of Jesus. Pilate had finally given in to the demands of the chief priests and the crowd and answered their cry for Jesus to be crucified. We will pick up in Luke 23. Start today by reading all the verses at once from 26-39. Then answer the questions that follow:

According to verse 26, who was seized to carry the cross for Jesus?

I don't know if this Simon knew who Jesus really was, but can you imagine what an honor and privilege it would have been to carry the cross for Christ? I can't imagine a higher calling in life, can you? Did you know that we have the same calling that Simon of Cyrene had?

Turn to Luke 9:23 and write what Jesus said that we all must be willing to do to follow Him.

I love the symbolism represented in this passage by the task Simon of Cyrene had. Simon carried the cross physically; we are to do it spiritually—which sometimes may involve an outward physical manifestation. We are told by Jesus that if we wish to come after Him, we must deny ourselves, take up our cross daily, and follow Him.

What a high calling this is, but what exactly does it mean? What does the verse say we must do if we wish to come after or to follow Christ? We must _________________ our self.

Why would this be important? As we discovered a couple weeks ago, we must live the crucified life. We are no longer slaves to sin. We must put away living for our fleshly desires and wants and live for what the Spirit of God wants instead. We must follow His leading and not our own.

How often are we to take up our cross?

Yes, we are to take up our cross daily and follow Jesus. It does take a daily submission to His will and His ways. Start your day by making yourself and the Lord verbally aware that you are submitting to His ways and carrying that cross. Acknowledge Him each morning as Adonai, your Lord and Master, and tell Him that no matter what the cross is for that day, you will carry it.

Now return to verses 27-31. While Jesus was on His way to the cross He spoke to the women who were mourning and lamenting Him, and He told them not to mourn for Him. Jesus does not want our sympathy, though it is hard for us to not have sympathy for Him. Jesus wants our faith. When He spoke to these women in verses 29-30, He foretold the destruction of Jerusalem and referred to the Great Tribulation.[10]

According to verse 32, who else was going to their death?

Verse 33 tells us that they came to a place referred to as "The Skull," and it was there that they crucified them, one condemned man on Jesus' right and the other on His left. Now let's look at the continued abuse toward Jesus while He was suffering on the cross. Look up the following verses and write what they did in front of and to Jesus *while* He was hanging on the cross:

Verse 34

Verse 35

Verse 36

Verses 37-38

Verse 39

Review yesterday's homework, remembering what Jesus went through *before* going to the cross. Now read your list above of what He endured *while* on the cross.

Keeping all that in mind, read and then write what Jesus said in verse 34.

Stop right there, and let His words sink into your mind. What does this statement say to you about the love and forgiveness of Jesus Christ?

To put it simply, for me, the sum of it would be, "The love and forgiveness of God and Jesus Christ His Son knows no bounds."

Did you know that while He hung there on the cross, our past, present, and future sins that put Him there weighed upon His shoulders? He loves and cares for you that much. He was willing to die for us because this was the perfect plan all along. Jesus was sent by His Father in Heaven to come and walk among us, to live among us, and to die for us. He hung on that cross for you and for me so we would be reconciled with God and so that we could live eternally in heaven with Him someday. What a precious gift from our heavenly Father.

Let's look deeper into this statement made by Christ. Jesus said, "Father, forgive them; for they do not know what they are doing" (Luke 23:34).

The Greek word for "forgive" is *aphiemi,* and it means "to send forth, lay aside, leave, omit, yield up."

How could Jesus—as they beat, persecuted, mocked, ridiculed, scourged, spit upon, slapped, and accused Him—say this to the Father?

Read Nehemiah 9:17 for the answer. What kind of a God is He described as? List all the adjectives.

I hope you picked up on the word *forgiveness* in all His attributes listed. He is a God of forgiveness. This is why Jesus could be taken to the cross and, while abiding with and praying to His Father, say, "Father, forgive them; for they do not know what they are doing" (Luke 23:34).

This brings us to the question we need to continually ask ourselves: If Jesus Christ could forgive them for nailing Him to the cross, how much more should I be willing to forgive?

It is part of God's very nature to forgive. It is who He is. Have there been sins you thought were unforgivable? There is only one thing that God cannot forgive, and that is unbelief. Those who do not believe that His Son, Jesus, was sent as their very own Savior have hardened their hearts against Him and denied His lordship; they will spend eternity separated from God. (This is also known as blasphemy against the Holy Spirit; see Matthew 12:31-32; Mark 3:28-29; Luke 12:10.)

For now, let's focus on allowing God to speak to us about forgiveness. What was the worst sin you committed, the one you wrote about yesterday or that you are too ashamed to write or think about? Did you know that Jesus has already taken that sin upon Himself? Did you know all that is required of you is for you to go to God with a heart of repentance—willing to turn away—and ask Him to forgive you? Have you? _________ If you haven't, or didn't yesterday, then do it now and write your prayer out to the Lord. Then thank Him that there is nothing that He will not forgive you for. ____

____

____

____

____

Don't ever ask for forgiveness for this sin again. It is done. He has forgiven you, and you need to move on. If you find yourself reliving this same sin, punishing yourself, or condemning yourself, then know that this is not from God, but rather from the Evil One. Read Romans 8:1 below.

"Therefore there is now no condemnation for those who are in Christ Jesus."

Allow God's forgiveness to overwhelm you and comfort you with the peace that surpasses comprehension (see Philippians 4:7).

Forgiveness: He so freely gives it to us, yet we have such a hard time giving it to others. Do you have people in your life whom you have never forgiven? Think on this one long and hard.

The issues could go back to your childhood or be something that happened just a few years ago. Whatever these things are, let God speak to your heart, and write all (no matter how many) of them out below.

This is a good exercise to do every now and then to keep your heart pure. Sometimes we have unforgiveness in our hearts, and we don't even realize it. Sometimes it is only made known through our actions toward another. Can you think of anyone whom you act a little short or rude with? If so, check your heart and make sure you are not harboring unforgiveness toward this person. At times this is how God will work to bring it to your mind. Other times it takes seeking God's quiet voice as we sit before Him, asking Him very directly if we have things in our lives that we have not forgiven. Don't let busyness keep you from doing for others what God so freely does for you.

Close today by writing your prayer of thankfulness to God for what He has revealed to you. ____

____

____

____

____

____

DAY 3: *An Exception*

Yesterday we studied Christ's example of forgiveness. Today we want to continue to study forgiveness and what God has to say about it. I cannot wait for you to see the blessing that God has for you today. Pray right now for His tender touch to go deep within you to help you understand the depth of His forgiveness. We will continue reading just a little further while still focusing on His time on the cross. Today we will pick up in Luke 23 again, but this time we will read verses 39-46. After reading this passage, answer the questions that follow.

Based on your insight into verses 39-41, what is the difference between the two criminals hanging on each side of Jesus?

After reading verse 42, what do you know about this one sinner hanging on the cross beside Jesus?

What did he say to Jesus?

What was Jesus' response to Him?

This is the magnitude of God's forgiveness. Please do not miss this. This one man was a criminal, and by his own words he stated, "We indeed are suffering justly, for we are receiving what we deserve for our deeds" (vs. 41). While hanging on the cross beside Him, he came to believe in Jesus as the Savior of his sins. Now let's look a little closer. Jesus was hanging there because of this criminal, because of the other criminal, and because of us as well. He hung there suffering from pain, but also from the fact that He who knew no sin *had become* sin on our behalf, so that we might become the righteousness of God in Him (see 2 Corinthians 5:21). Besides suffering out of physical pain; as if that were not enough, Jesus suffered because He had to bear the sins of the world. Jesus, who knew no sin and who had walked among us without sin, was now carrying the sins of the world. Yet, while suffering in this way, He said yes. What did He say yes to? He said yes to taking yet another's sins upon Himself so that this one person would spend eternity in heaven. Read the poem below to give you further insight.

You Said Yes

You said yes while in Your pain,
You said yes so that this one would gain.

You said yes while You suffered so,
You said yes because You couldn't say no.

It is not in Your nature to reject.
A sinner turned is a sinner kept—

Kept from the darkness and the fiery pit,
To dance in Your presence and suffer not a bit.

You never would choose for any to depart,
To live without You because of a hardened heart.

You said yes, because You couldn't say no,
To this thief on the cross, for him to go.

Thank You that Your yes, to me implies,
The endless limits to Your tries.

That even for one You would agree,
To hang a little longer on that ol' tree.

While in the depths of Your physical pain,
You chose to hang longer for another to gain—

To gain an eternity with You he will live,
Because You continued to love and forgive.

Even heavier still is the grief You bore
When Your Father turned aside, You to ignore.

The sins that weighed so heavily upon Your back
Remind me often that I will never lack.

To have Your forgiveness each time I ask,
Thank You, Jesus, for completing the task.

You died for all upon that tree,
But You would have hung longer even for me.

Thank You, Jesus, for saying yes,
You gave us Your all and nothing less!

Lori Merrill
February 13, 2003

Jesus hung there for the criminal who did not choose Him. He hung there for the one who did. He hung there for both of their sins, but one believed and the other did not. The magnitude of God's love and forgiveness is incomprehensible! Do you agree? He hung there for you before you said yes. Though He knew who would someday say yes and who wouldn't, He hung there so that *all could!* I can't help but praise Him for that right now! Praise Him with me:

Lord, we thank You for suffering for us, for carrying our sins upon Yourself for us. Thank You for Your love that knows no bounds, and thank You for Your example of forgiveness through Jesus Christ, Your Son and our Savior! Amen!

Let's talk about the one who did not choose to believe that Jesus was His Savior. What do you think happened to him?

Scripture is clear that those who do not receive Christ as their personal Lord and Savior will spend eternity separated from the presence and love of God. This is the one exception to God's forgiveness. Look up the following verses and then write what each one says about this place of separation from God.

Matthew 25:30

Matthew 25:46

Mark 9:43

Mark 9:47-48

Luke 16:22-31

To have anyone I care about have to spend eternity separated from God is an almost unbearable thought for me. To have to think about *anyone* having to spend eternity in suffering and separation from our Father is unbearable also! I pray that you can point to a time when you invited Him to be the Lord of your life and asked Him to forgive you of your sins. If you have not ever asked Him to be your Savior, or if you have any doubt, please do not move forward without making sure. You see, Christ forgives because He knows our need. In fact, He looks past the sin and straight to the need. He sees our need for a Savior. Our need is Him. That is why He so freely gives. Do you remember the time when you acknowledged your need for Him, asked Him to forgive you of your sins, and invited Him to be the Lord of your life?

If so, then praise God for that! And if you haven't, will you now? God has made it so simple for us. We simply must believe, confess with our mouth that Jesus is the Son of God, and acknowledge Him as our Savior (see Romans 10:9-10). Thank Him now for His nature of forgiveness. Pray for Him to give you more of a nature like His.

God saw past the thief's sin and straight to his need. I ask you, could you do the same?

Those people who have hurt you, whom you have not forgiven, or who are hard to forgive: Can you look past their issues and be like Christ and see their needs? They need a Savior just like you do. I have a friend who once told me that every time she told her dad about a mistake she made, he would say, "That's why we need a Savior." Think about it. These people in your life are imperfect just as you are. And just as you and I need a Savior, so do they. I am not implying that they are not Christians, because they may be. We all sin. But no matter what level of spiritual maturity we have reached in our Christian walk, we will still need a Savior. The good news is that we have one. We have one who is ready and so willing to freely grant us forgiveness each time we ask.

If Jesus can forgive you for all that you have done, are doing, or will do, how can you not forgive others?

Close today by spending a few moments asking God to give you the desire, courage, and perseverance to forgive as He does. Then thank Him for what He is about to do in your life!

DAY 4: *Satan's Attempt*

If I were ever forced to name a recurring lesson in my life, it would be forgiveness. For reasons I will never comprehend, I have had to live it since a young age. Through events that could have led me to a life of bitterness, God has molded me, transformed me, and made me more like Him. I find myself over and over again learning to go to an even deeper level of forgiveness with the passing of the years. There are, no doubt, others who have had more painful things occur in their lives, as well as others who have experienced events that would be harder to forgive. Yet, I believe that God has allowed me to experience an array of hurt at a variety of levels so that I am able to comfort others in their sorrow. This is also so that I could walk that path and teach others about His goodness, His faithfulness, His forgiveness, and His love that knows no bounds! It has not been an easy walk. I didn't always feel or act Christlike. Yet I would do it all again to experience Him and to know Him like I do. The result of Christlike forgiveness is that we bring honor and glory to His name. I pray that through this week's lesson you will see that the one purpose in writing it is, and will always remain, that He be glorified. The Lord is worthy and deserving of *all* praise, honor, and glory! Invite Him now to do a mighty and powerful work in your life today.

Today we are moving to another story and example of Christ's forgiveness. Read Luke 7:36-50 and then answer the questions below.

Jesus is at a Pharisee's house having a meal, and who joins them uninvited?

What did she do (vs. 38)?

I love how Jesus always knew what people were thinking. No one had to say a word or give a look; He knew their thoughts before *they* knew their thoughts. This Pharisee named Simon was judging this woman. He probably thought Jesus was absolutely nuts for allowing her to be there, cry over Him, wipe His feet with her hair, and anoint Him with the perfume. Why do you think this woman was crying?

Have you ever been so broken by the realization of your sins that you can empathize with this woman?

I have. When I realize the magnitude of my sinfulness or the grief that it causes God, there are times that I just "lose it" like this woman did. I wish my sins always brought that kind of grief from me, because then I would be less likely to sin so often. I believe that a repentant child of God is precious in God's eyes because He sees our hearts. Sometimes when I can't express my grief properly over my sins, I just cry; yet I know that the Holy Spirit is taking every thought, every inch of grief, and presenting it to my Lord in a manner that can make sense to God. When I cannot speak, He does it for me. Then Jesus is there relaying it as well, interceding for me on my behalf to the Father, sharing with Him my hurt, my pain, and my sorrow. What a precious sight for me to imagine: the Father and the Son talking about me, discussing my brokenness and my regret. The thought of it gives me great comfort. Have you ever thought about the Father and the Son talking about you? Allow yourself to imagine the scene and write what They would be saying right now.

When I ask you this, I realize that you are probably like me, and you think of all the bad. But don't! It is like looking at a picture of ourselves. Rarely do I look at one without immediately noticing all the flaws and thinking, "Oh yuck!" Yet, that is not how God sees us. Read Psalm 139:17-18: His thoughts toward us are very different than what we may think they are.

"How precious also are Your thoughts to me, O God! How vast is the sum of them! If I should count them, they would outnumber the sand."

God does delight in us! So think positively about what He and the Son would be saying about you right now!

Getting back to the story, why was this Pharisee so appalled at Jesus?

What did he see about the woman that he thought Jesus didn't know?

Did Jesus know all about this woman and her sins?

What would you say (based on verses 40-47) is the difference between this woman and the Pharisee?

If you had to choose one of these two people, the Pharisee or the woman, which one would you say you are most like?

Hopefully we all are like the woman sometimes, but if we were honest, we have a tendency to be more like the Pharisee.

Think about the difference between Jesus and the Pharisee. What would you say is the primary difference?

I hope you said something about the fact that Jesus knew this woman's heart and the Pharisee judged her by the actions he had seen. The one lesson that I have learned over and over is that Christ was able to forgive because, besides being part of the Trinity, He has the ability to look past our actions and straight to our need. I have touched on this all week, but now I want to hit you with it straight on. Jesus looks at the need; we look at the actions. Herein lies the difference between Him and ourselves. Jesus sees the need for a Savior; we see the sin. Haven't you ever wondered how Christ could forgive like He did and does? Have you ever wondered why God forgives so readily? The answer lies in what He can see. You have to understand that God knows our need. Our deepest need is to be reconciled with Him—we need a Savior! He sees past our circumstances and sees straight to our need. Our deepest need and longing is for Him!

We, too, should be able to be like Christ and forgive. Read Ephesians 4:32. According to this verse, how are we to forgive?

Would God tell us to forgive like Him if we couldn't?

Read 1 Corinthians 2:16. Based upon the truth of God's Word, whose mind do we have?

Read Matthew 6:14-15 to find out what God says about our unwillingness to forgive others. What did Jesus say would happen if we did not forgive others?

I truly believe that part of God's plan is to allow things in our lives so that we can learn to forgive and have just a taste of what it was like for Him and His Son. If we could not relate at some level, then we wouldn't have an appreciation and gratitude for His gift of forgiveness. I also believe that the Lord allows us to experience the need to forgive others so that through our forgiveness people may see God in us. Sometimes, our forgiving heart toward others is what God will use to draw them to Himself. Pray that you will be that one who extends forgiveness so that others see Christ in you.

Read 2 Corinthians 2:10-11 below:

"But one whom you forgive anything, I forgive also; for indeed what I have forgiven, if I have forgiven anything, I did it for your sakes in the presence of Christ, so that no advantage would be taken of us by Satan, for we are not ignorant of his schemes."

This word translated as "forgive" and "forgiven" used in this Scripture is the Greek word *charizomai*, which means "to grant as a favor, to give freely, to bestow." We must freely extend our forgiveness to others just as Christ did for us. How dare we hold back from anyone what Christ so freely gave to us. How can we claim any right to not forgive when He has forgiven us for all things? And He has forgiven the other person before they even ask. I can remember so vividly years ago when I was in what I have labeled as the "trial of my life." While I was crying out to God about the hurt, the betrayal, and the pain, I remember repeating over and over again, "Lord, I can't believe they did this. I will never be able to forg—," "I can't believe someone would lie about something like this. I will never forg—," "How could anyone be so irresponsible with other people's lives. I will never be able to forg—." No matter what was said, He would not let me finish the sentence. I wanted to say that I would never forgive this one particular person, but every time I started to say that word, the Holy Spirit would stop me and then a thought—His prompting—would come to me. He would impress this upon me: "Lori, I have forgiven you for everything you have ever done in your past, the sins of your present, and anything that you will do in the future. How could you dare think that you could not forgive this person?" That was all it took. I never did finish the sentence. The thought would come, but He would not let me say it. I had no right. I gave up all rights when I surrendered to Him as my Lord and Savior.

Read 2 Corinthians 2:11 again.

"So that no advantage would be taken of us by Satan, for we are not ignorant of his schemes."

There are several points to take notice of in this verse.

1. **Satan will try to take advantage.** We have studied many tactics of Satan, and one of the things we learned in battling him is how very important it is to know and believe God's Word. Trust God when He warns that Satan will take advantage of our unforgiveness. If we do not forgive, Satan will make use of that for his good and our demise. This word translated here as "advantage" means "to get an advantage, defraud, make a gain." I believe with all my heart that a little unforgiveness goes a long way! Satan will use it to his advantage and take even that little bit and make headway with destruction. Even a hint of unforgiveness in our lives and Satan will make it grow like a weed. He will sprinkle thoughts here and there until a root of bitterness grows. Then he will add water (more thoughts) and fertilizer (anger and wrath). In fact, if he gets it going well enough, he doesn't even have to tend to it. We do a good job helping it bloom from that point on!

2. **Satan does have schemes.** The word *schemes* means "mind, thought, purpose, mind games." This is what he is best at. He will keep planning schemes in your mind and in your thoughts until he finds one that works. That is why it is so important to "Philippians 4:8" all your thoughts.

   According to this verse, what things are we to dwell upon? ______________________
   ____
   ____
   ____

   I have a good friend who always says, "If a thought does not pass the Philippians 4:8 inspection, then you march that thought right up to the throne of God and give it to Him." This has always given me a great visual of what I need to do with unwholesome thoughts. We must take such thoughts captive to the obedience of Christ (see 2 Corinthians 10:5). Remember, greater is He who is in me than he who is in the world (see 1 John 4:4)!

3. **Forgiveness is important so that our relationship with God is not harmed.** When I realized this truth some years ago, it was what drove me to strive to forgive. I love my dear heavenly Father, and though a great injustice had been done to me and my family (the trial of my life), God lovingly reminded me that if I didn't forgive, it was not that person who would suffer, but rather it was my relationship with Him that would be harmed. This was not a price that I wanted to pay. And though I did not feel like forgiving, I also did not want to walk through years of my life only to look back and say, "That was when I strayed from the Lord." Please realize how vital this truth is. I am so glad that He reminded me of this in the midst of my grief. I can still remember saying to a dear friend, "I will forgive, no matter what it takes out of me, because I love the Lord too much to let my relationship with Him suffer." Think about it. Why let what someone else has done to you make you suffer the greatest pain of all: A Christian who lives life out of fellowship with their Lord.

Finally, we need to realize that Satan's desire is for us to not forgive anyone. However he may accomplish this makes no difference to him, as long as he keeps us from forgiving as Christ does. Remember God's plan is for us to become conformed to the image of His Son. If we are holding a grudge, unforgiveness, and bitterness in our hearts, then we are not conforming to the image of Christ. That is why Satan wants us to focus on another's actions rather than their need for a Savior. I want to stress once again our need to follow Christ's example by looking past the sins of another and to their needs. If our eyes are on the action or sin, then we are not using the mind of Christ that we have been given. Stop right now and write your prayer to God, asking Him to make you very aware of *any* and *all* unforgiveness within you. Then thank Him that we truly can forgive as He does! ____

____

____

____

____

____

DAY 5: *God's Gift*

Today we want to get down to the nitty-gritty of forgiveness. We want to leave this week behind knowing that we have looked in every nook and cranny of our hearts and allowed the Holy Spirit to clean out all the fresh dust and old cobwebs. My prayer is that when you finish this week, you will feel renewed, refreshed, and transformed by the Word of God, letting Him invade every part of your being. I pray that each of us can be like the sloth in the movie *Ice Age*, who said, "I am too lazy to hold a grudge!" Rather than it be because of laziness that we don't hold a grudge, let it be because of Christ that we are able to forgive as He does.

Let's return to our story once more. Skim Luke 7:36-50 again and then focus on verse 47. Finish the statement that follows: "For this reason I say to you, her sins, which are many, have been forgiven, for she loved__________________; but he who is forgiven little, loves ______________________."

Do you love much or little?
Have you been forgiven much or little?

No matter what we have done, we all have been forgiven much. Some of us have a lot more junk that we bring to the table when we meet Jesus, but even so, we all have been forgiven much. We deserved to pay the price of sin, but Jesus paid it for us. The question is: Are we aware of *how much* we have been forgiven? Read the verses below.

"When you were dead in your transgressions and the uncircumcision of your flesh, He made you alive together with Him, having forgiven us all our transgressions, having canceled out the certificate of debt consisting of decrees against us, which was hostile to us; and He has taken it out of the way, having nailed it to the cross." Colossians 2:13-14

What did Jesus forgive us of?

How much of our transgressions?

What did He cancel for us?

What did he do with the certificate of debt?

Let's ask the question again: If Jesus forgave us for all our transgressions, then what right do we have to not forgive another?

Prayerfully read the questions below and then look up the verses that follow. Write your answer to each question after reading the verse.

How do you feel when you have been forgiven? (Psalm 32:1)

What is my responsibility, and what will God then do? (Psalm 32:5)

What does God do for me? (Psalm 65:3)

What does God offer to me, and what does He have for me? (Psalm 86:5)

Does God always forgive, and what must I do? (1 John 1:9)

What if my brother keeps sinning against me? (Luke 17:3-4)
How often do I have to forgive another? (Matthew 18:21-22)

How do I treat those who have hurt me? (Romans 12:14, 19-21)

Before we close for today, please pray and ask the Lord if there is anything that He needs to reveal to you through the verses you just read. If during the course of this week God has laid on your heart that you need to seek forgiveness from another for a hurt that you caused, I pray that you will be prayerful, obedient, and faithful to do just that. Write your commitment to the Lord now. ____
____
____
____
____
____

We will close this week with verses that I highly recommend you memorize, especially if you are currently dealing with the difficulty of forgiving someone. Pray through these verses on your own behalf and personalize them by inserting your name as you pray.

"So as those who have been chosen of God, holy and beloved, put on a heart of compassion, kindness, humility, gentleness and patience; bearing with one another, and forgiving each other, whoever has a complaint against anyone; just as the Lord forgave you, so also should you. Beyond all these things **put on** ***love, which is the perfect bond of unity. Let the peace of Christ rule in your hearts, to which indeed you were called in one body; and be thankful."***
Colossians 3:12-15

God bless you!

Week 6

Jesus: His Example of Confronting Others

"And while being reviled, He did not revile in return; while suffering, He uttered no threats, but kept entrusting Himself to Him who judges righteously." 1 Peter 2:23

Day 1
Is It Necessary?

Day 2
A Clear Purpose

Day 3
Motives Are Essential

Day 4
Properly Put

Day 5
Oh, That Tongue!

Memory and Meditation: "Let your speech always be with grace, as though seasoned with salt, so that you will know how you should respond to each person." Colossians 4:6

Prayer: *Dear Lord, we praise You, Father, for Your faithfulness to us even when we are faithless. Thank You for Your love that knows no bounds. Thank You for being patient with us though we are not always patient with You or with others. Lord, we pray this week that You continue to show us ways in which we can become more like Your Son. Lord, we pray for our lives to reflect You always. We pray for lives lived in such a way that others are drawn to You. We know that You can do this through confrontations with believers and nonbelievers as well. Teach us, Lord, when and when not to confront others. Lord, teach us how to confront in love with pure motives and for the purpose of restoration and peace. Lord, once again we pray that You mold our lives this week to reflect the example of Your Son.* **Amen.**

Week 6

Jesus: His Example of Confronting Others

"And while being reviled, He did not revile in return; while suffering, He uttered no threats, but kept entrusting Himself to Him who judges righteously." 1 Peter 2:23

DAY 1: *Is It Necessary?*

I realize that this may be a very challenging lesson for many of you. I would imagine that you are either on one extreme or the other regarding confrontations: You either have them or you don't! For most of us, there is no in-between. We are either a go-tell-them-what-I-think person, or we believe that we shouldn't ever say a negative word to anyone. May I kindly suggest (with only a slight confrontation) that if you fall on either extreme that you are mistaken?

Jesus did confront! In fact, Jesus was a very confrontational person, and we want to learn from His example. We want to look at His example to learn how He would want us to confront. Jesus was also a nonconfrontational person at times. He passed up confrontations that were hard to understand. When I read about the times He turned away or refused to answer, I am convicted by His self-control and my lack of it at times. Some of you might have been swayed to do this Bible study when you read that this topic would be a part of it. I understand. There was a time in my life when I would have taken a Bible study for the sole reason of learning what God's Word says about how to confront another. It is that hard for some, and it used to be for me as well. I cannot say that it is easy yet, but at one time in my life I would not do it at all. I thought that as Christians we were to let everything roll off our backs and move forward. But through years of experience I have learned that I am not only disobeying God, but I am doing that other person and myself no favor at all when I avoid a confrontation.

We see through God's Word that Jesus confronted a lot! We also see through God's Word that Jesus chose not to confront at times when the situation was the most heated. Today we will first take a look at some of the times that Jesus chose not to confront. Before we do, read the statements below about confronting others. Circle the statement(s) that best describes you.

I never confront, no matter what the situation is.

I sometimes confront, but it has to be pretty bad before I get to that point.

Sometimes I do and sometimes I don't, depending on the situation.

I hate to confront, but I do when I have had enough.

I don't plan to confront, but when I do, I explode.

If someone has done wrong, I say what is on my mind, no matter what.

I always confront others who have hurt me.

I don't know where you are on the spectrum, but if you are like me, you can relate to all of the above to some degree. As I stated before, for years I had somehow come to believe that as a Christian I should never confront, no matter what. The problem with that type of thinking is that it is so unscriptural. God's Word is very clear that there are times when we are to indeed confront others. What are we to confront about? We are called at times to confront others about sin in their lives, or about some way in which they have offended us. The problem with my old belief of never confronting was not in the confronting itself, but with my definition of what confronting another meant or would "look like." You see, if we have never had positive examples in our lives of confrontations, then we probably have a wrong idea of what they are to be like. For me, a confrontation meant a fight. I didn't know that there could be another way. So, if you asked me about confronting another, I would have likened it to having a fight, strong emotional disagreement, or argument with another. Confronting as Jesus did is based on a whole other definition. The difference is our purpose, motives, and how we confront another—all of which we will study this week. Based on what I have just shared with you, think about your own personal definition of a confrontation and write it below.____

____

____

____

Out of curiosity, and to clarify exactly what we are studying this week, I used the Webster's dictionary to look up the definition of *confront*. There were two options for this word. The first meaning listed is, "to face, especially boldly or defiantly." The second listed is, "to bring face-to-face (with)."[11] When I speak of Jesus or us confronting another, it is definitely not defiantly, though it may require being bold. We will define a confrontation this week as "bringing an issue face-to-face."

All this week we will look at many confrontations between Jesus and others. For now, let's focus on Scripture about Jesus and His examples of *not* confronting. Look up the Scriptures below and briefly describe the circumstance that Jesus was in and how He responded. Make note of whether this situation was a peaceful or hostile environment.

Matthew 12:14-16

Luke 4:28-30

John 6:14-15

In all the situations above, Jesus chose not to confront others. He chose to walk away from the situation or out of the situation rather than confront others about their actions or thoughts. Why do you think Jesus chose to turn away?

Now look up John 18:28-38. Read these verses, noting to yourself how many times Jesus answered Pilate and whether He removed Himself from the situation. After reading the Scripture, answer the questions below.

Could Jesus have removed Himself from this situation? When answering this question, don't forget Matthew 26:53 where Jesus states that He could appeal to His Father and His Father would at once send twelve legions of angels.

What do you think was the difference in Jesus choosing not to remove Himself from this situation while the other times He avoided a confrontation and even left the scene?

Let's dig a little deeper to find out the answers to these questions. We will begin first in Isaiah 53. Read verses 4-6 of this chapter, knowing in advance that this is the foretelling of Jesus Christ, what He would someday do, and what He would someday endure.

After reading Isaiah 53, read the following verses and note beside each one what Jesus said would someday happen.

Mark 10:32-34

John 12:32-33

Now read the verses in John 8:28-29. According to these verses:

- Who is Jesus obeying?
- When Jesus speaks, who has told Him to speak?
- Who is Jesus living to please?

If Jesus did nothing on His own initiative, how much more should I live in this way?

According to all we have read today, do you think that there are times God wants you to confront another and there are times that He doesn't?

How will you know the difference?

All is based on God's timing and God's plans. Jesus did it all according to His Father's leading and His Father's perfect plan. We have learned from our previous weeks' lessons that nothing can thwart the plan of God (see Isaiah 14:24, 27). This was God's plan for His Son. Because Jesus abided continually with the Father, He knew when to remove Himself from a situation. Jesus knew *what* His Father wanted Him to say and do and *when* He wanted Him to say and do it.

Can you say the same for your life?

Have there been times that you confronted when you were to be silent, or stayed in a situation when you were to leave?

What was the result?

If Jesus needed to obey the Father's guidance for the "right time" to leave or stay, how much more should I?

I would guess that if you remember the situation, then the result might have been disastrous. If so, ask the Father's forgiveness now and be willing to do whatever it is that He wants you to do to make things right.

We have seen today that God's perfect plan for His Son prevailed even in the midst of times when it seemed that it would not. Jesus abided with His Father so that He would live life according to His Father's plan and live a life that pleased His Father. You and I want the same.

We will close today by reading two verses from Proverbs. Read the verses below and answer the questions that follow.

"He who conceals a transgression seeks love, but he who repeats a matter separates intimate friends." Proverbs 17:9

"A man's discretion makes him slow to anger, and it is his glory to overlook a transgression." Proverbs 19:11

Now relate this to our own lives. Do these verses tell you that there are some things that you should overlook?

It isn't always necessary to confront, is it? Sometimes we forgive (conceal) a transgression without confronting. Jesus didn't always acknowledge his adversaries' accusations, nor did He always confront wrong. Many times He turned away. Let us be like Christ in this area. We must abide with the Father so that we will know His plan as to when we should confront others or turn away as Christ did. God bless you for seeking His will!

DAY 2: *A Clear Purpose*

Today we will switch gears and begin to study some examples of when Christ did confront others. I have learned so much from the Scriptures in this area of my life. Confronting others is never easy. If it is something you enjoy then I would question your motives and purpose in doing so. No matter how many times God calls me to confront another, I don't think I will ever enjoy it. The only joy that comes out of it for me is to know that I have obeyed the Father. If He allows us to see the "fruit" of our obedience then there is almost nothing like it. I would never want to imply through this week's lesson that I am an expert on this subject, because I am far from it. I do have a wealth of experiences though. Many are negative and ones that I would rather forget; others are positive and situations that I would readily recall. What is most important to me is that you allow God to take this part of your life and speak to you about the way He would desire to change you. You may be one who confronts too often and not in a Christ-like way. Or you may be one whom God has given the gift of discernment but you don't follow through on what He has called you to do when He calls you to do it. No matter where you are, stop right now and invite God to have every part of you today. Ask Him to make you receptive to what He wants to teach you.

The first point that I want you to understand is that each time Jesus confronted another, He had a clear purpose in doing so. Because Scripture does not always tell us what Jesus or God was thinking or intending, we don't always know the purpose behind the confrontation. I would never assume to know every purpose or intent behind each confrontation either. I am very aware that God's ways and thoughts are above my own (see Isaiah 55:8-9). However, many times we are allowed to see some of the purposes behind the confrontation. As I have stated before, I believe that God in His perfect will has multiple purposes behind each plan—many of which we will never see or know until we get to heaven. As I have studied God's Word and Christ's examples, I have come to believe that *Jesus always had a purpose for confronting another.* Today we will look at two purposes for Jesus' confrontations.

1. To bring glory and honor to God

Let's first look at one confrontation that Jesus faced and dig into Scripture so that we can learn from His example. Read Mark 2:1-12 and then answer the questions below.

According to verse 5, what did Jesus see in these four men?

What were some of the scribes doing while Jesus spoke to the paralytic? (vs. 6)

Did they say these things out loud or just think them? (vs. 8)

Jesus knew in His spirit that these men were thinking this to themselves. What do you see as the difference between the paralytic and his friends compared to the scribes?

In verse 8, Jesus chose to confront these men about their thoughts. Can you imagine how this might have blown you away if you were one of these scribes? Jesus knew exactly what these men were thinking and then asked them a question about their thoughts. Then in verses 10 and 11, He tells them the reason He is doing these things. What does Jesus say is His reason in verse 10? "So that you may ____________ that the Son of Man has authority on earth to __________________ sins."

Everything Jesus did was intended to bring honor and glory to God. Read verse 12 and note what happened after the paralytic picked up the pallet and went out in the sight of everyone.

Describe the action of the people.

Who were they glorifying?

What were they saying? "____"

In this example of Jesus' confrontation, we see that His plan was to bring honor and glory to God. This is always Christ's plan and should be ours as well. From this passage of Scripture, we don't know what the scribes' response was, however, we do know that all who witnessed the paralytic walking were amazed and glorified God as a result. You see, Jesus was performing this miracle to draw others to Himself—which would bring them to the Father. Every healing that Jesus did while on this earth was for the purpose of bringing attention to the Father. As Jesus brings the Father attention, the Father receives the glory which only He deserves. How sad that the scribes couldn't see God *through* the healing. Instead, they were too caught up in seeing and judging the action and statement.

We cannot rely on another's response to our confrontation to bring honor and glory to God. We are only responsible for ourselves and for being obedient. If we have felt called by the Lord to confront another about their actions or lack of actions, then we will know that we have brought glory and honor to God from our obedience whether we see it or not! But what if our confrontation does result in a righteous response? What do we do then? Read Matthew 5:16 below for your answer.

"Let your light shine before men in such a way that they may see your good works, and glorify your Father who is in heaven."

Who do we want to receive the glory?

We always point men to God no matter what. Our responsibility is that others do not worship us, but worship God instead. We want Him alone to be glorified as they respond and turn to Him.

2. To bring restoration

The second purpose of confrontation should be to bring about restoration. Now we will look at another of Christ's confrontations—one that led to restoration. The story we will read is a well-known confrontation between Jesus and a little man who climbed into a sycamore tree. I can already hear the song in my head, can't you? Read Luke 19:1-10 and then answer the questions below.

Who is this man?

What was his job?

How does the Bible describe his financial status?

What did Zacchaeus do to be able to see Jesus?

Why did Jesus want Zacchaeus to come down?

When Jesus told Zacchaeus to come down, what was his response (vs. 6)?

What did Zacchaeus tell Jesus he would do (vs. 8)?

Based upon the crowd's response (vs. 7) and Zacchaeus's offer to give back four times as much, do you think it is likely that Zacchaeus cheated people?

What was the end result of this confrontation?

What did Jesus say that the Son of Man has come to do in verse 10?

Jesus stated in verse 9 that salvation had come to this house. Zacchaeus had met his Maker and Creator, and his life was dramatically changed forever. What a sweet and precious story of a heart coming to see Truth, and by meeting Truth, his life was changed in a moment. The confrontation was with Truth. That is what God can do.

Now let's apply what we are learning. Has God ever called you to witness to another and you saw this type of dramatic change? If so, write about it, and thank Him for it. _________

____

____

____

Now let's get a little more personal. Has God ever called you to directly confront a brother or sister in Christ about their sins? If so, did you, and what was the result? _______

____

____

____

If you haven't ever confronted another about their sins then answer this question: Have you ever seen a brother or sister in Christ do something sinful or turn to sin, and you grieved for them and wanted to say something, but didn't? Why or why not?

You may have thought it was none of your business or you were too uncomfortable to say anything, or you simply turned your head because you didn't want to get involved. The fact of the matter is that God may have allowed you to notice a sin in another so that you would confront for the purpose of restoration in this person. You and I both know that sin gone unchecked begins to take over in our lives. It could happen quickly, or it could happen over a matter of years. But there are always consequences to sin that are left to rule in our lives. It may start out small, but you can bet the enemy doesn't intend for it to stay small. Whatever your reason for not confronting another about their sin, prayerfully consider the truth found in the following Scripture.

Read Matthew 18:15-17 to determine what God wants us to do about sin in another's life. Now write out the steps below that Jesus has given us regarding how to confront another in sin.

1.

2.

3.

4.

This is where living the Christian life can be very difficult. We want an easier way out. I know that there have been many times that God has prompted me in this area and I start looking for any excuse to *not* have to do the steps above. It is hard. Now you plainly see why it was so important to learn about obedience before we came to this lesson. More importantly, to learn about living an abiding life so that we could know that it is indeed God calling us to confront. The important thing to remember is that we are to be obedient to God's call. If He has called you to confront someone, then you are to do it and not worry about the outcome. Your job is to be obedient, and the other person's job is to receive the words from you and weigh them against their actions and before the Lord. You are not responsible for their response. Let me say it again: You *are not* responsible for their response. You are only responsible for what the Lord has told you to do. What they do in response is between them and the Lord.

We will stop here today. This is a lot to think about. Let's close with a couple of Scriptures to encourage you and for you to think about.

"Do not reprove a scoffer, or he will hate you,
Reprove a wise man and he will love you.
Give* instruction *to a wise man and he will be still wiser,
Teach a righteous man and he will increase* his *learning." Proverbs 9:8-9

"Therefore, to one who knows the right thing to do and does not do it,
to him it is sin." James 4:17

Write your thoughts before the Lord and record anything He has revealed to you. ______
____
____
____

DAY 3: *Motives Are Essential*

Today we want to begin to examine our motives behind a confrontation. We know that Jesus would, of course, always have pure motives. What about our motives? To be able to confront another as God leads us, we need to be sure that we have pure motives. So, today in our lesson, we will examine some of the stumbling blocks to having pure motives. We need to always be willing to check ourselves against God's Word to make sure that we are first doing what God has called us to do, and also whether our motives are pure behind that calling. In today's lesson we will examine what we need to avoid when faced with confronting another.

Our purpose should be, as stated yesterday, to bring honor and glory to God and to bring about the restoration of another. Our motives behind a confrontation can be difficult to judge on our own. As we have learned from Scripture, the heart is wicked and deceitful above all else, and we should not trust it (see Jeremiah 17:9). So, how does one know that their motives are pure? We need to check ourselves against three things.

1. Judgment

It can be very easy to see another's sin, can't it? Sometimes we see another's sin before we are aware of our own. God warns us against judging another. Read Matthew 7:1-5 and answer the following questions:

Why does Jesus tell us to not judge another?

What did Jesus say would happen to us if we judged another?

Finish this statement: "By your standard of measure, it will be ______________________ ___________ ___________________."

What strong word does Jesus use to describe a person who stands in judgment of another?

We looked at this word in our very first week of study. This word *hypocrite* means an actor or pretender. In other words, a person who pretends to be something he or she is not. Jesus is telling us in very strong language to not stand in judgment of another. Of course, by His use of this word, He is implying that the one who judges is not what he or she seems, and thus not in a place to be making a judgment of another.

What did Jesus tell us we need to do before we look at the speck in our brother's eye?

I believe, if you are like me, that these few verses have kept you from going to another when you might have felt called or prompted to do so. Jesus is warning us to not try to judge as God judges. As my father-in-law recently told me, we are only capable of being "fruit inspectors." God is the only one who can judge another because God looks at the heart. We look at the outward actions. We can never presume to know another's heart. That is something only God can do. Read Jeremiah 17:9-10 on the following page.

"The heart is more deceitful than all else and is desperately sick; Who can understand it? I, the Lord, search the heart, I test the mind, Even to give to each man according to his ways, according to the results of his deeds."

If we can't even trust our own hearts, then how can we assume we know another's? We can't, but God does! That is why we must make sure it is God who is prompting us to go to another. We must make sure that we are only seeing their actions of sin. We cannot think we know their heart! It may be something that someone said that you need to question further, or it may be the actions that you see in them that displays to you their sin. We must never confront their intention. In fact, their intention might have been quite innocent. We can only confront what we know and see from them. We are never to presume to know their heart or the intention behind the action or statement.

Hear what I am saying—no one person belongs on a pedestal in your eyes except God alone.

Once again, our job is to be obedient and trust God to do the work "behind the scenes." If He calls you to confront, then He will give you the power and strength to do so. And if our hearts are right with Him, then we will have the pure motives that we should have.

2. Unrealistic Expectations, Jealousy, or Envy

The second thing that we need to check our hearts against is placing unrealistic expectations on people. We need to make sure that we are not quick to point out another's flaws because we are jealous or envious of this person. This can easily happen when someone is being used by God in mighty ways. I have noticed that once God begins using someone in powerful and wonderful ways, all of a sudden we as Christians put that person on a "platform of perfection." This person usually has no idea we have put them there in our minds. However, because we so admire or see the work of God in their lives, they have risen to this platform that we will *not* let them step off of. If they step down, then we are ready and waiting—not to catch them—but to watch them fall. Sometimes we do this because of our admiration toward that person, and sometimes we do it because we are envious. If it is because of admiration, please be so careful. People who are being used mightily of God do not want the kind of admiration that places them on a pedestal. They will someday fall, and most likely you will too because of your disappointment in them. Take it from someone who has made this mistake more than once, God will find some way for that stool to be knocked out from under them—in your eyes. I thank Him for this. It has taken some hard and tough lessons, but I am so thankful for these lessons. Hear what I am saying—no one person belongs on a pedestal in your eyes except God alone. In my naivety, I put people there and then when they would disappoint me (even without them knowing it), I would fall with them. God has taught me over and over again that it is okay to respect and admire them, but it is unhealthy to put them on a throne that only He belongs on!

The other thing we need to guard our hearts against is jealousy or envy. We need to make sure we are not quick to point out another's flaws because we are jealous or envious of them. Maybe it has to do with the attention they are getting or because we think they have some secret connection with God. Whatever the reason, when we are envious or jealous of another, we sit waiting to watch them mess up. Or we look for anything imperfect in their lives that we can latch onto so that we can find fault in them. Be on guard against these motives. I have personally witnessed envy and jealousy drive people to great lengths to destroy, manipulate, and hurt others. Read below what God's Word has to say regarding this subject.

"Wrath is fierce and anger is a flood, but who can stand before jealousy?" Proverbs 27:4

You might be thinking that Christians wouldn't do that to one another. Friend, could I say to you that Christians are human also? Think about it: That is why we have a Savior and why we still need to go to Him asking forgiveness frequently. We need to abide in Him so that our hearts remain pure before Him. Read below what Paul wrote about those who were hurting him because of envy.

"Some, to be sure, are preaching Christ even from envy and strife, but some also from good will; the latter do it out of love, knowing that I am appointed for the defense of the gospel; the former proclaim Christ out of selfish ambition rather than from pure motives, thinking to cause me distress in my imprisonment." Philippians 1:15-17

If God has called you to confront another about sin in their life or some way they have offended you, then make sure you have checked your heart against envy, jealousy, and unhealthy admiration. Any of these would be indications that you are seeking to find flaws in another because you have unreasonable expectations of them.

3. Vengeance

The third motive we need to guard against is vengeance. Hurtful actions against us are possible reasons to confront another only as long as it isn't to pay them back for what they did. It would be appropriate to go to another to confront them for their sins because their actions were hurtful against us. However, to hurt them back would never be appropriate, though that is what our sinful nature might desire to do. This is an area we have to be particularly careful about. "Pay backs" can be deadly for the offender and the one offended. This would never be God's plan. Remember, if we are going to another to confront, we are seeking to restore and to reconcile rather than to hurt them or to get back at them.

Read the Scripture below and answer the questions that follow.

"Never pay back evil for evil to anyone. Respect what is right in the sight of all men. If possible, so far as it depends on you, be at peace with all men." Romans 12:17-18

According to these two verses, what are we never to pay back?

What are we to seek if at all possible?

"Never take your own revenge, beloved, but leave room for the wrath** of God, **for it is written, 'VENGEANCE IS MINE, I WILL REPAY,' says the Lord. 'BUT IF YOUR ENEMY IS HUNGRY, FEED HIM, AND IF HE IS THIRSTY, GIVE HIM A DRINK; FOR IN SO DO-

ING YOU WILL HEAP BURNING COALS ON HIS HEAD.' Do not be overcome by evil, but overcome evil with good." Romans 12:19-21

What are we to never take?

Based upon these verses, what are we to leave room for?

What does God say that He will do?

What are we to overcome evil with?

God's Word is very clear. We are never to return evil to another or take our own revenge. In fact, God states that vengeance is His, and He will repay. Our natural reaction to someone hurting us is to take revenge or to want to hurt them back. If you are like me, you can handle someone hurting you, but someone hurting those you love is a whole different story. But God says to leave room for His wrath. In other words, our sovereign God knows the best way to teach them a lesson. We may never know how or when, but our job is to trust Him and obey Him!

The best advice I can give against vengeance is to be a tattletale! Go straight to your heavenly Father just like you would your daddy. He is your Abba Father, your Daddy. Go to Him, and tell Him all about what they did to hurt you. Tell it all, every single bit of it, every hurt and every detail, and then let Him be your avenger in the way He plans. Then trust Him in it. Also remember that confronting another's wrong actions does not mean you are taking revenge. Your job is to make sure that your confrontation is not done out of vengeance, that you are not doing it to hurt them in return. We can honestly and lovingly confront another about how they hurt us without doing so in revenge (we will get to this tomorrow). Read the psalm of David below as he cried out to God about his enemies.

"Contend, O LORD, with those who contend with me;
Fight against those who fight against me." Psalm 35:1

God will take care of His beloved children. He is our Shepherd, and He loves us dearly. He has plans that we will never understand. Our job is to trust Him in those plans. His ways are always better than our ways!

I clearly remember being in such a state of shock and pain during a trial in our lives that I knew I couldn't trust my actions. I was so numb from the pain and grief of betrayal that I knew it wasn't wise to trust my actions or my emotions at that point in my life. I remember praying the following Scripture every day and with each move that God called me to make.

"Search me, O God, and know my heart;
Try me and know my anxious thoughts;
And see if there be any hurtful way in me,
And lead me in the everlasting way."
Psalm 139:23-24

I prayed this prayer every day for almost a year until I knew that my frame of mind was trustworthy. I did not want to make a wrong move, and with each move that I felt called to make, I fervently prayed this Scripture. I also told the Lord to keep me from anything that would be a mistake. In other words, I reminded God often that He knew my heart, and if I was doing something out of His will (though I was seeking His will desperately) then He needed to somehow stop me from going forward.

You see, God wants the best for us, and He wants the best for that person He is calling you to confront. We must remember that Christ's purpose is to bring honor and glory to the Father and to restore the one who may be straying or is lost. To be like Jesus we must examine our motives so that they are pure, just as Christ Himself is pure. We must guard against the stumbling blocks of being judgmental, jealous, envious, having unrealistic expectations, or taking revenge. When we feel the nudge of the Holy Spirit, then we need to respond. And as long as we are examining our actions in light of God's Word, then we will be well on our way to bringing glory to Him and possibly restoring a brother or sister in Christ!

DAY 4: *Properly Put*

Today we will begin to examine the actual confrontation. We will look at how we go to another to share with them what God has placed upon our hearts to tell them. I always say, "what God has placed upon our hearts to tell them" because there should never be a confrontation that was not preceded by prayer. Sometimes one can see a sin so clearly that there is no doubt that we must confront, but we still need to precede it with prayer. We want to seek the Lord about when, how, and where to confront another as well as about what words to use. Prayer is so very important not only for *our* actions, but also for the recipient's actions. We need to pray that our hearts are pure, as we have studied this week, but it is also very wise to ask God to prepare our brother or sister's heart as well. Ask God to bestow favor upon you in their eyes, and ask Him to make their heart hungry for Truth.

Today I want us to read the well-known confrontation between a prophet of God and a man who was known as "a man after God's own heart" (see Acts 13:22). When we think about David and how blessed he was by God, we either think about one or the other: His close times with the Lord or his sinful time out of fellowship with God. David is a great example of what can happen to any of us when we stray from keeping God as our focus and priority. In 2 Samuel 11 the story begins by stating that it was spring and this is the time when all the kings go out to battle. At this point David chose to stay home from battle, and when evening came he walked around on the rooftop. From his viewpoint David could see a beautiful woman bathing. Instead of fleeing from the temptation right then, David indulged himself. He inquired about her and sent for her. As the story goes, the woman (Bathsheba) became pregnant by David though she was married to another man. David, in an effort to cover his sin, had her husband killed in battle and then brought Bathsheba to his house to become his wife. This is where the confrontation between Nathan and David begins. Please read 2 Samuel 12:1-14 and then answer the questions below.

Nathan tells David a story. What is David's reaction to the story (vs. 5)?

What did David tell Nathan should happen to this man as a result of what he had done?

In verse 7 Nathan then announces what to David? "You are the ___________!"

It then takes Nathan verses 7-12 to relay all the sin that David has committed and what the Lord is going to do. What was David's response to all of this in verse 13?

Can you imagine what David must have felt like? Think about how angry he was by the story and how his response was that this man who had taken what was not his deserved to die and should also make restitution fourfold. He was outraged by the actions of this man. Then imagine the moment that Truth caught up with David. In his mind, all of a sudden he realized that he was indeed the thief, manipulator, betrayer, adulterer, and murderer. He was indeed the rich man who had stolen from a man who had little. David had all he could have ever wanted, and God would have given him more (vs. 8)!

Now go back to verse 1 of this story and write the very first sentence.

Who sent Nathan to David?

This brings us back to the first point I made in today's lesson: *We must seek God before we confront another***.** Scripture is clear that we should confront another in their sin. However, we must seek God's leading, timing, words, and wisdom. Nathan was a prophet who was called by God to confront David. Today we have the blessing of having the Holy Spirit within us to speak to us about our sin. Does this mean that God will never call another to confront you about your sin? No, it does not. God may use another person because you are in denial of your sin, indulging yourself in it, or so blinded by the sin that you have quenched the Spirit from revealing it to you. I believe that God does indeed give wisdom and discernment even today through other Christians. I believe that He does this because He loves us so much and because the body of Christ is to be a support and encouragement to one another. Oh, how I wish we could all learn this. We are to support and encourage one another! With this support and encouragement comes great accountability to one another. This is *agape* love. It is not judgment of another. Hear me out: If confronting another in their sin is done properly, it is not being judgmental of another; it is a loving concern for another's spiritual walk so that you don't watch them fall into sin as a habit of their life. Read the following verses, noting the answer to each question below the verse.

Proverbs 18:19
Why should we be careful and prayerful when confronting another?

1 Corinthians 4:21
How should I confront another?

Galatians 6:1

In what way do I confront, and what do I need to check?

This last verse is a little difficult to understand. As I sought the Lord about this verse, He was faithful to reveal to me what He is warning us against. In the recent past, the Lord called me to confront a sister in Christ about a sin He had made evident to me over and over again in her life. I was struggling about the call to confront this friend. I was asking the Lord to remove the burden from me if it was not from Him. (I really wanted it removed even if it was!) With each prayer requesting the removal, God, through His sovereignty, placed me in a position where I would witness this person committing the same offense against others. This was reaffirming the burden to confront. When I finally did confront this sister in love, the Lord allowed me to experience this verse firsthand. My friend and I discussed what the Lord had laid upon my heart and all was fine. She was truly sorrowful for what she had done.

Soon after this confrontation, I noticed that I was tempted to slip several different times into the same sin that I had confronted her about. I do not fully understand it, except to say what a heyday the enemy would have for me to fall in this area, especially after I had just confronted a friend about her sin. Wouldn't it be just like our adversary, the Devil, to lay such traps for us to fall into? What kind of a testimony would I be if I turned around and sinned in the same manner? I also believe God may be speaking of our humility in Galatians 6:1 as well. He tells us to look to ourselves so that we will not be tempted. In other words, I believe He is warning us against *thinking ourselves above* committing this particular sin. Humility—how important it is, especially when confronting another.

This brings us to our second subject of the confrontation: *Facing another about their sin must be done in humility and love*. We spent a whole week on the subject of love, and there was a reason we had to learn about love before we could talk about confrontation. I want to remind you of 1 Corinthians 13:1-3. Read it before going on.

"If I speak with the tongues of men and of angels, but do not have love, I have become a noisy gong or a clanging cymbal. If I have the gift of prophecy, and know all mysteries and all knowledge; and if I have all faith, so as to remove mountains, but do not have love, I am nothing. And if I give all my possessions to feed the poor, and if I surrender my body to be burned, but do not have love, it profits me nothing."

These few verses remind us of the fact that no matter what we do in life, if it is done without love, then it is useless. There is no eternal value in what we say, give away, know, or sacrifice if these are not done in love. The same principal applies to confronting another. How could we ever think we could approach another about a sin without our actions and words dripping with love? People will see the love of Christ through you whether they want to face their sin or not. In fact, let me offer you something to think about: *If you see someone you truly care about falling into sin or sinful behavior, how much love are you expressing by turning your back and pretending it isn't there—because you did not want to face them with it?* It is because of this love for them that you would and should confront them. I believe this is *agape love*! I also believe this was the intention of the Lord when He told us to support the body of Christ and build one another up. Read Ephesians 4:15-16 below:

> ***"But speaking the truth in love, we are to grow up in all aspects into Him who is the head, even Christ, from whom the whole body, being fitted and held together by what every joint supplies, according to the proper working of each individual part, causes the growth of the body for the building up of itself in love."***

According to these verses, how do you think confronting another about a sin would benefit the body of Christ?

I remember reading an article recently about two Christian friends. One woman shared with her friend her attraction to another man and how unhappy she was in her marriage. The other friend, obviously uncomfortable, changed the subject and never asked her another thing about it. The first friend ended up having an affair with the man and suffered a long time from her sin and the devastating effects of it. She wondered what might have happened if her friend had confronted her about her early confession. Would she have stopped? Would she have heeded her advice? She was not blaming her friend, for she knew the responsibility was hers, but I cannot help but ask you if you have been in a similar situation?

Have you ever had someone whom you felt you should have spoken to about a sin or possible sin in his or her life and you didn't?

If so, looking back on it now, do you wish you would have said something?

Do you feel like it was the Lord prompting you to say something?

Given all that you have studied this week up to this point, how might you handle the same situation differently?

The important thing to remember is that confronting another could be God's way of working through you to pull another back to Himself and to build up the body of Christ. The body of Christ is in desperate need of being built up from within. We are also in desperate need of being a good example and godly testimony to the unbelieving world. I think the following verses will provide more guidelines about facing another. Look up each verse and write some of the helpful guidelines that are given which would be beneficial for you to remember about confronting another.

Matthew 7:12

Philippians 2:3-4

2 Thessalonians 3:15-16

Romans 12:9-10, 16

The final verse to remember in all situations when confronting another would be John 3:30. May this become a life goal of all of us in any and all situations.

"He must increase, but I must decrease."

Just as everything we have studied these last five weeks should lead others to Jesus Christ, so should a face-to-face confrontation. The way we handle ourselves in this situation and the way we live our lives should draw others to Him. If we are willing to be an empty vessel to be used by Him, then He will use us in confrontations with Christians and non-Christians. Before we close today, spend a few minutes thinking about how your definition or perspective of a confrontation has changed. Write your thoughts on the lines below and then ask the Lord to continue to teach you about this subject. God bless you!

____
____
____
____
____

DAY 5: *Oh, That Tongue!*

I think it would be very unwise of me to write a week of lessons on confrontation without focusing at least one day on the tongue. We have studied together what God's purpose for a confrontation is, what our purposes and our motives should be, and how we should confront another. Now we want to look at the words we use. Since a confrontation has everything to do with what we say and how we say it, I want us to spend today focusing on that small part of the body that can be so very powerful!

We want our words to be carefully chosen by God. Though we are coming face-to-face with someone about actions, behavior, or words that may be ungodly, we still want our words to reflect Christ. We can give advice and reprove someone and still be a source of encouragement and love. There are multitudes of Scriptures on the tongue.

Read the following and write beside each one how this would apply to confronting another person.

Romans 14:19

Proverbs 18:21

Matthew 12:36-37

Ephesians 4:29

We all agree that this can be hard. However, remember the following if you are tempted to pass up this assignment from the Lord:

- It can be just as damaging to not confront another who is in sin. It could express a lack of concern for them or allow them to remain in the sin longer.
- You are not responsible for how they receive it or how they respond. You are only responsible to obey. You may have to remind yourself of this truth over and over again as you are preparing for the confrontation.

Hopefully the following steps will be helpful in a future confrontation.

Practical Tips about Confronting Another

Set an appointment. Make an appointment to meet for lunch or to get together to talk. If possible, let them know that you have something you need to talk to them about. This keeps you accountable to obey the Lord. It also helps to keep them from being caught totally off guard. Once you make the appointment, I would suggest it not take too long between the time you make the appointment and the actual date of it. Meeting somewhere to have food, coffee, or tea helps to make it a more relaxed and comfortable atmosphere. There are times that this would not be appropriate. Sometimes the issues to discuss have to be said and then you must separate. Use wise judgment on where you should meet and for how long you want to be together. If the issue is very private, personal, and even emotionally charged, it may not be good to meet in a public place. All of this would, of course, depend upon the issue being confronted.

"Commit your works to the Lord and your plans will be established."
Proverbs 16:3

Always try to have a confrontation face-to-face. This allows them to see your emotions and your intentions in a way that they may not be able to otherwise. If you cannot do it face-to-face, then at least do it on the phone. The last resort would be a written confrontation, and I would say that you should only do this if they refuse to meet with you or listen to you over the phone. If this is the case, then you need to make sure that you are still supposed to confront them. If you are, then pray about having a godly counselor or mentor read the letter (if they do not know the person) to make sure your wording and intention is clear. The problem with the written word is that it can be easily misinterpreted. It could have much love behind it, but others may misinterpret it because they don't hear your tone. Never send an anonymous letter or note. This is a cowardly approach and one that does not allow that person to ask questions of you.

"If your brother sins, go and show him his fault in private; if he listens to you, you have won your brother." Matthew 18:15

Write down the information or the particular situation that you are confronting. This will help you to stay focused and not forget important details if you are nervous. You can even tell the person that you made some notes as the Lord led you to and you may be referring to those as you talk. If you do this, make sure it isn't a list of "wrongs" that the person has committed. This is more for you in case you are nervous or have trouble staying focused.

"Anxiety in a man's heart weighs it down, but a good word makes it glad." Proverbs 12:25

Pray with the person before you begin if possible. Many times I have asked the person or people whom I am with if I can pray before we begin. I always pray that God would guide and direct our conversation and that nothing said would be misinterpreted. I also ask that my words would be seasoned with grace and bring honor and glory to Him. This is another way that people will see our hearts. If we are sincere in this prayer then they will see it, hear it, and witness it firsthand.

"The tongue of the wise brings healing." Proverbs 12:18

Precede with praise. Encourage the person before beginning. Tell them what their relationship or friendship means to you. Sincerely give them encouragement or praise about how important they are to you personally or to the situation that is involved.

"Pleasant words are a honeycomb, sweet to the soul and healing to the bones." Proverbs 16:24

Focus on action and not the person's character. Always focus on the person's actions and not their character. As we discussed before, we cannot judge their intentions; we can only go by what we see in their actions. Keep focused on the act itself, and do not get sidetracked by your perception of their action. Never attack their character.

"The one who guards his mouth preserves his life; the one who opens wide his lips comes to ruin." Proverbs 13:3

Stay focused. This is very important to be aware of before going into a face-to-face confrontation. Some people, out of self-defense, may turn the tables on you and your actions. If this happens, it is wise to remind them that they do have a responsibility to share that with you, but this is not the time. You also can gently remind them that they have never come to you about what they are bringing up, and if they felt strongly about it, then they should have. Tell them that right now you are doing what you feel led by the Lord to do and you need to keep focused on that. Then stay on the subject at hand.

"When there are many words, transgression is unavoidable, but he who

restrains his lips is wise." Proverbs 10:19

End with your affirmation of them. After you have said all that you feel you should say then close with your concern, care, and love for them. Tell them that you will be available to them (if this is appropriate) and that you will pray for them. If possible, pray with them before leaving. Allow them to respond to all you have said, but if they do not respond then don't force their reaction.

"He whose ear listens to the life-giving reproof will dwell among the wise." Proverbs 15:31

Be prepared to react. Your reactions during the confrontation is so important. You may be surprised by the reactions you get from people you confront. They may shock you with anger, tears, silence, or lack of concern. Hopefully you will get a very positive and remorseful reaction that leads to reconciliation or repentance before the Lord. Whatever their reaction, yours is even more important. Pray that no matter what they say, you will react in a godly way. You need godly wisdom to deal with their reaction.

"The heart of the righteous ponders how to answer, but the mouth of the wicked pours out evil things." Proverbs 15:28

Please realize that I am not in any way condoning that we run to a brother or sister in Christ to confront every mistake he or she makes. I am not. We are not to be the moral police for the Christian body. However, if we see a brother or sister in Christ who is sinning in such a way that God has prompted us to confront, then we need to apply the principles of Matthew 18:15-17 in a prayerful manner. We also need to realize that with this accountability to others comes an individual accountability as well. We have the responsibility to receive admonishment in a godly manner as well. I hope that each of us is in a place in our lives that we would truly want to be loved and accountable to this extent.

I have come to believe that if more Christians confronted one another, then many of the sins that we see so rampant in the church would diminish to a great extent. I have watched many Christians share with one another what one person is doing to hurt them without ever going to the one who is doing the hurting. Think about gossip or hurtful words that a particular person repeats over and over again to many people. Don't you think that if their brothers and sisters in Christ confronted them about their hurtful actions, then this person would have to face their behavior one way or another?

I have also watched God do a miraculous work in lives that were obedient and willing to confront. Unfortunately I have witnessed far more people sit by and watch as their family members, friends, or brothers and sisters in Christ live a life of disobedience because they don't want to get involved or offend someone they love. How dare we care more about offending a fellow human being than offending our heavenly Father through disobedience!

Please do not decide I am radical without spending time in His Word and before Him in prayer on this subject. I believe what I have shared with you is from personal experience—good and bad. I have failed to obey, and I have obeyed and failed. I have failed only in my attempts with a godly confrontation because I did not allow the Spirit to lead me. You must make a choice.

Will you obey God's Word or not? God's way is always best! God's Word is *always* true! Why would we do anything other than His way?

How has God spoken to you this week? Write your prayer or thoughts to Him below.

____

____

____

____

____

____

We will close this week's lesson with a section of Scripture that seems to bring it all together:

"To sum up, all of you be harmonious, sympathetic, brotherly, kindhearted, and humble in spirit; not returning evil for evil or insult for insult, but giving a blessing instead; for you were called for the very purpose that you might inherit a blessing." 1 Peter 3:8-9

Week 7

Jesus: His Example of Compassion

"Seeing the people, He felt compassion for them, because they were distressed and dispirited like sheep without a shepherd." Matthew 9:36

Day 1
A Pharisee's Flaw

Day 2
Compassion on Display

Day 3
Compassion Withheld

Day 4
Compassion in Action

Day 5
Christ's Compassion

Memory and Meditation Verse: "So, as those who have been chosen of God, holy and beloved, put on a heart of compassion, kindness, humility, gentleness and patience" Colossians 3:12

Prayer: *Lord, I thank You, Father, that You have brought us to this point in our study of Your Son. What a delight this has been. Thank You for the opportunity to study the examples of Jesus. Lord, change us just a little bit more this week so that we reflect the image of Christ. Speak to our hearts about compassion. Teach us what it means to be moved by and feel compassion as Jesus did. Give us wisdom to listen and obey when You call us to act. Open our eyes to the many opportunities to serve You and others with a heart of compassion. Lord, remove any hardness in our hearts and replace it with a tenderness and love that seeks to please You by reaching out to others.* **Amen.**

Week 7

Jesus: His Example of Compassion

"Seeing the people, He felt compassion for them, because they were distressed and dispirited like sheep without a shepherd." Matthew 9:36

DAY 1: *A Pharisee's Flaw*

God never ceases to amaze me. On my first day of in-depth study and writing of this week's lesson, I sat down at the breakfast table to lead a devotion for my children. The Lord then directed me to get out one of our previous devotional books from the hidden shelf in our coffee table. I walked over, lifted the top, and picked the first book I saw from the many we keep there. I chose a devotion about Christian martyrs from the book. After finishing the devotion, I slowly skimmed through the book. There, right before my eyes, was a whole section devoted to compassion, including the best definition I had come across to explain compassion. The section even referenced some of the examples I had planned to use. Though I had made a page of notes and references of Christ's examples of compassion, I had been praying about how to explain it. God, in His faithfulness and goodness, had answered my prayer before my writing even began!

I have been blessed by the example of Jesus and His expression of compassion toward others. Some time ago, I began underlining and highlighting in my Bible each time I came across a Scripture that displayed Jesus' feelings of compassion. We know that Jesus loved others, and we know that we are to do the same. But what about compassion? Why is there a distinction in Scripture between the times Jesus demonstrated compassion and the times He expressed love? This was the question I had been grappling with for some time. According to the devotional I read my children, "Many of us feel pity, sorrow, and concern when we see the needs of others, but a compassionate person channels those feelings into action. Compassion is *caring enough to become involved in meeting someone's needs*. Jesus was often moved by compassion."[12] We want to follow His example.

Let's begin today by reading a profound statement made by Jesus to the Pharisees. Begin reading in Matthew 9:9-13 and then answer the questions below.

Who was dining with Jesus?

What did the Pharisees ask the disciples?

Jesus heard what they asked of His disciples and said to them, "It is not those who are healthy who need a physician, but those who are sick" (vs. 12). What do you think He meant by this statement?

By making this statement, I believe Jesus is indicating that His ministry is for those who realize they have a need. The Pharisees did not see themselves as sinners, so they would not have sought out Jesus as their Savior. Why do you think the Pharisees did not see themselves as sinners?

Jesus then tells them to go and learn what something means (vs. 13). What did He want them to find the meaning of? "I desire compassion and not _______________."

What do you think this statement meant, and why would He ask this of the Pharisees?

The Pharisees always behaved properly. They followed the Law to a T! I believe they saw their life as a life of sacrifices—sacrifices that involved the things they should not or could not do in addition to always bringing the proper animal sacrifices to the Lord. The Christian life is not about dos and don'ts. In fact, if we are living it in this way, then we are missing the vital part of the Christian walk—the relationship of the Christian life. Jesus does not want it to be about sacrifice. In fact, He desires love, mercy, and compassion instead of sacrifice.

Can you think of a time when you have felt you were sacrificing for God by the things you don't do?

Have you judged others on their Christian walk based on what they don't do?

Let's go a step further. Have you assessed another's spiritual level based on what they don't do?

I'm sure we have all done this to some extent. We need to be very careful to guard against legalism. The Christian life is so much more than "don'ts"!

Jesus is telling the Pharisees that satisfying the Law is not good enough. We can be legalistic and fulfill the rules, but what if we are missing the intent of the rules? Read Mark 12:29-31. I know we have looked at this before, but once again, according to Jesus, what are the two most important commandments? To love the Lord God with all your ____________, ____________, ____________ and ______________. And to love your ____________ as yourself.

Based on your studies and all you know about the Pharisees, were they obeying these two commandments?

The Pharisees were interested in keeping the Law. They thought by keeping laws they were loving Him. They were not interested in loving God or others. They thought it was about rules (sacrifices) instead of love and mercy (compassion). Jesus was trying to get the message through to them that it is about relationships, not rules. Their very flaw was that they thought they had no flaw! According to one commentary, "The Pharisees always brought the proper sacrifices, but they were totally lacking in compassion toward sinners. When *mercy* is lacking, then religious formalities are meaningless" (cf. Hosea 6:6).[13]

I could so easily look at my service to Him as a sacrifice and therefore get so caught up in the details that I don't have compassion or express compassion to all those around me. The Lord wants more than that from me. He wants my compassion toward others. He desires for me to reach out and care enough to become involved in people's lives.

Have you ever justified not meeting another person's needs because you are so busy doing "other things" for the Lord?

Let's close today with a prayer. Ask the Lord to make you aware of any area in your life that you have been like the Pharisees or you have become too busy to extend compassion. Ask the Lord to reveal legalism in your life to you. Now sit and listen, and write down anything He has revealed to you. Then obey Him! ____

____

____

____

DAY 2: *Compassion on Display*

Today we want to begin our study by looking at some examples of Christ's compassion on display. Go to the Lord in prayer, asking Him to prepare your heart to be changed as we study His Word and the example of His Son, Jesus.

Look up each Scripture, noting what Jesus felt and then what He did in each situation.

1. Matthew 14:14

Jesus felt:
Jesus responded:

Now read Matthew 14:6-14 to get the full story of what happened.

John the Baptist has just been beheaded, and the disciples told the news to Jesus. After hearing about John, Jesus withdrew from there in a boat to a secluded place to be by Himself. Jesus was in mourning. He loved John, and though He knew that this was God's predetermined plan, it didn't hurt any less. Although Jesus must have been enduring much grief over the death of John, He didn't let this stop Him from meeting needs. He put others' needs before His own.

2. Matthew 20:34

Jesus felt:
Jesus responded:

Now read Matthew 20:29-34 to get the full story of what happened.

In this situation there is a large crowd following Jesus. Sitting by the road are two blind men who begin yelling for Jesus. Based on what they are yelling, do you think they believe in Jesus as the Son of God?

The crowd tries to quiet them down, but instead they cried out even more, and probably louder. Then Jesus stops to ask them what they want. They tell Him that they want their eyes to be opened. How did they address Jesus?

Jesus touched their eyes and immediately their eyes were opened. Then what did these men do?

3. Mark 1:41-42

Jesus felt:
Jesus responded:

Now read Mark 1:39-42 to get the full story.

A leper has either heard of Christ or has seen from afar that Jesus is preaching and casting out demons. He comes to Jesus, beseeching Him, falling on his knees, asking Him if He is willing to make the leper clean. Think about the faith in that statement. He did not ask Jesus if He could. He asked Jesus if He was willing, and if He *were* willing, then he told Jesus that He *could*. No wondering about it. In one statement he told the Lord that He knew He could cleanse Him—all He needed to do was to be willing to cleanse him. Jesus touched the leper. This move in itself would make the crowd gasp; lepers were made to live away and stay away from everyone. They were even required to yell about their condition so others walking toward them would know to keep their distance. Can you imagine how humiliating this would be? The amazing thing here is that Jesus touched him. I can just imagine the gasps of the crowd as Jesus walked up to this man and reached out and touched him. This man had probably longed to be touched, yearned for a human's touch, ever since contracting leprosy. Isn't it just like Jesus to go a step further? He could have spoken the words to heal this man as He did with so many others, instead, He stretched out His hand and touched him, and the leprosy was gone in a moment!

4. Mark 6:34

Jesus felt:
Jesus responded:

Now read Mark 6:30-34 to get the details of the story.

Jesus was trying to get the apostles away from the people for some much-needed rest. Many saw them going away in the boat, and wanting to see them so desperately, they ran ahead from many cities to get there before them. Jesus goes ashore and sees the large crowd waiting.

Why does Jesus feel compassion for them?

What does He do with that feeling of compassion?

Jesus met their need for a Shepherd by teaching them. They were hungry for the Word, so He taught them. He saw their need to know Truth, and He met their need.

The above stories state that Jesus felt compassion and that He was moved by compassion. Both phrases, "felt compassion" rand "moved by compassion," are from the same Greek word, *splagchnizomai*. This word means "to be moved in the inward parts." In other words, Jesus so felt this compassion that it moved Him to do something about it. Recall our description of compassion from yesterday: "Many of us feel pity, sorrow, and concern when we see the needs of others, but a compassionate person channels those feelings into action. Compassion is *caring enough to become involved in meeting someone's needs*."[14]

How about you? When you see something that brings out the mercy in you, what do you do about it? When those feelings come to the surface, do you stifle them? A compassionate person channels those feelings into action instead of stuffing them. Can you think of a time when you had pity, sorrow, or concern about another and then you stifled or shelved your feelings? If so, what was the situation and how did it make you feel?

Many of us feel merciful toward another. We feel for their situation or difficulty; we hurt with them. However, compassion is a step further. A compassionate person gets involved and meets the need. In all the above stories, Jesus met needs. He was grieving, and He put that aside to meet the needs of the people. He saw blind men, and He was willing to stop and heal them. He saw a man with leprosy, and He reached out and touched Him to heal him. He saw a crowd of people who needed to have a Shepherd, and He began teaching them.

If Jesus was willing to care enough to get involved and meet needs, shouldn't I be willing as well?

Read the Scripture below:

"Just as the Son of Man did not come to be served, but to serve, and to give His life a ransom for many." Matthew 20:28

How does the above verse reinforce what Jesus did?

What about you? What has the Lord allowed you to see the need for?

Maybe it is helping someone who is ill. Maybe it is teaching a group that needs a shepherd. Maybe it is reaching out to love someone who needs a special touch. Will you be willing to get involved in that ministry God is calling you to? Most likely, if the Lord has prompted you over and over, then it is something He wants you to get involved in. Maybe you are fearful or feel unqualified. Friend, if the Lord is calling you to it, then you *are* able—if you are willing. God will supply all you need.

"And my God will supply all your needs according to His riches in glory in Christ Jesus." Philippians 4:19

When He calls you to meet a need, He supplies all you need! You are not qualified, but He is through you! Just as Jesus was able and He told the leper that He was willing, you too will be able if you are willing. When you feel compassion, will you let that compassion move you to become involved in ministry? Will you be like Christ and say, "Yes, I am willing!" If so, then write your prayer to Him now. ____

____

____

____

____

God will bless your compassionate heart!

DAY 3: *Compassion Withheld*

Today we will dig into God's Word and read about a time when compassion was given to one and withheld from another. Pray before you begin and ask the Lord to make your heart ready to hear from Him.

We are starting in Matthew 18 today. Jesus has just been asked by Peter how often he should forgive his brother for sinning against him. Peter asks if he should forgive seven times. Jesus replies by telling him it is seventy times seven, and then Jesus tells him a parable which starts in Matthew 18:23. Read the parable (verses 23-35) and the comments below, and then answer the questions that follow.

The king realizes that one of his slaves owes him ten thousand talents. When the slave is brought before him, he cannot pay back to the king what he owes. The king was going to have him sold along with his wife and children to repay the debt. So the slave fell to the ground and prostrated himself and begged him to have patience, for he would repay. According to verse 27, what did the king (lord) do?

Did the king require him to pay back the debt he owed?

Think about this a minute. The slave asked that the king be patient so he could repay. Did the slave ever ask that the debt be forgiven?

Think about this in relation to God. He is our King and "the king" in this story. He didn't make a way for us to pay Him back for our sins. He completely forgave us (removed the debt) of our sins. Read Colossians 2:13-14 below.

"When you were dead in your transgressions and the uncircumcision of your flesh, He made you alive together with Him, having forgiven us all our transgressions, *having canceled out the certificate of debt* consisting of decrees against us, which was hostile to us; and He has taken it out of the way, having nailed it to the cross." (emphasis mine)

Praise God!

Pick up the story in verse 28. The slave went to find one of his fellow slaves who owed him a hundred denarii. What did he want of his fellow slave?

His fellow slave fell to the ground pleading with him, asking him to have patience, and telling him that he would repay. Now move to verse 30. What did this slave (who has been forgiven his debt by his lord) do to his fellow slave?

Now, some of his fellow slaves have watched what has happened, and they go and report all of this to their lord. (I am reminded of Numbers 32:23, "Your sin will find you out.") So, the king summons the slave, and there is quite a heated confrontation. Read again what the king says to this slave whom he has forgiven (vss. 32-33).

According to these two verses, what is the king so appalled by? The slave's lack of ________________. So what happened to the slave as a result of his lack of mercy/compassion according to verse 34?

Before we go on, let me share something with you that brings tears to my eyes. The king first forgave the slave of how much? ___________________________________The slave then goes to his fellow slave wanting him to pay him back how much? __________ ____________________ A denarius was a Roman silver coin, worth about a day's wages. A talent was worth about fifteen years' wages of a laborer.[15] Now remember, the king forgave ten thousand talents. Ten thousand is a plural word which could mean "ten thousand or countless, innumerable." This slave owed his lord ten thousand talents, and each talent is comparable to fifteen years' wages. I believe Jesus was making the point that this slave was indebted to his lord for countless debt. One couldn't keep up with it; it was so much debt that there would be no way to count it. Now relate that to us. We are the slave; God is the king in the story. We are indebted to God for innumerable sins, too many to count. We can't keep track. They are countless. Yet, He looked down upon us, extended His compassion to us, and forgave them all. He wasn't just patient with us to repay. He forgave us for all of our debt through the sacrifice of His Son!

Jesus finishes the parable by saying what? Fill in the blank: "My heavenly Father will also do the same to you, if each of you does not ___________________ his brother from your heart" (Matthew 18:35).

This is a story about forgiveness, for sure, but it is so much more than that. The king felt compassion toward his slave and forgave him completely of his debt. A person with compassion gets involved in meeting the need. Thank goodness we have a God who met our need. Thank you, Lord, for being a Lord of compassion! Scripture proclaims, "The Lord is compassionate and gracious, slow to anger and abounding in lovingkindness" (Psalm 103:8). He met our need to be forgiven. He extended compassion to us. He didn't just say, "Those poor humans, they sure do sin a lot. They need help." He looked past the sin (as we learned in our lesson on forgiveness) and straight to the need. Then, when He saw the need, He responded out of compassion. This is the thing about compassion: It will require something *of* us and *from* us. The requirement from God was the sacrifice of His Son. Compassion will require our time and our resources, but we want to be like Christ and be "moved by compassion."

When we stop and think about how compassionate the Lord has been to us and how we see Christ being so compassionate toward others, we must face our weaknesses. Has the Lord brought to your mind areas of your life where you have lacked compassion like the slave who was forgiven? Remember, you are that slave.

"Just as a father has compassion on* his *children, so the LORD has compassion on those who fear Him." Psalm 103:13

We have to be willing to love, forgive, and then get involved. Has the Lord spoken to you about areas that He has met your needs, yet you have been unwilling to meet another's? What has the Lord done for you that you have refused to do for others? Confess it to Him now through a written prayer. It is so very important that you do not skip this part or think it unimportant. Remember, the Lord wants to speak to you and to conform you into the image of His Son. Confess those areas now so that you will receive the compassion of the Lord. ______________________

____

____

____

"He who conceals his transgressions will not prosper, But he who confesses and forsakes* them *will find compassion." Proverbs 28:13

God bless you!

DAY 4: *Compassion in Action*

Today we will look at another of Christ's parables. Pray for a tender heart to hear from the Lord.

Our study begins in Luke 10—the well-known story of the Good Samaritan. Jesus has just been questioned by a lawyer, "What shall I do to inherit eternal life?" Jesus in turn asked the lawyer, "What is written in the Law? How does it read to you?" (Luke 10:25-26). This lawyer then responds with, "Love the Lord your God with all your heart, and with all your soul, and with all your strength, and with all your mind; and your neighbor as yourself" (vs. 27). Jesus tells him that he has answered correctly and then adds, "Do this and you will live" (vs. 28). The lawyer then asks one more question, wishing to justify himself: "And who is my neighbor?" (vs. 29). Now read Luke 10:30-37 and answer the questions that follow.

What did the priest do when he saw the beaten man?

What did the Levite do when he saw the beaten man?

What does it say in verse 33 that the Samaritan felt when he saw the beaten man?

How was the Samaritan different from the priest and the Levite?

List all the ways the Samaritan helped the man:

-
-
-
-
-

Out of the three people mentioned in the story, who can you most relate to?

In what ways?

The Samaritan became very involved. This act of mercy and compassion took a lot from the Samaritan. It took his time, his efforts, and his money. These are some of the things that few of us are willing to give, or we may want to give, but only when it is convenient for us. Convenience versus compassion: Which one wins most for you?

The Good Samaritan allowed action to follow his feelings. He felt compassion and mercy for the man, and he allowed those feelings to move him into action. Read the verses below and answer the questions.

"We know love by this, that He laid down His life for us; and we ought to lay down our lives for the brethren. But whoever has the world's goods, and sees his brother in need and closes his heart against him, how does the love of God abide in him? Little children, let us not love with word or with tongue, but in deed and truth." 1 John 3:16-18

According to the verses above, how do we know about love?

What are we to do for the brethren?

What does this verse say about us if we see a brother in need and ignore it?

Finally, how are we to love others?

Every love mentioned above is *agape* love. Remember the definition I wrote in our lesson on love: *Agape love reaches out to love when love isn't deserved or reciprocated, and does so without expectations*. So according to the verses above, if we see a brother in need, we cannot turn our back on him and ignore him, or we are not expressing *agape* love toward him. In other words, this is how God loves us (*agape*) and this is what God would do, so how could we not? We can say a lot about loving another. We can tell someone we love them until we are blue in the face, but *agape* love extends compassion toward them and shows it in deed and truth. If we are expressing *agape* love toward another, then we will automatically extend compassion to them!

We have to remain on guard against developing a cold and hardened heart. Why? So we will continue to express love and compassion toward others. We live in a world full of sin, and it is easy to develop a hard and calloused heart within us as a result of all the hurt and suffering in the world. We can also develop a heart like this by building a wall of protection for ourselves that refuses to reach out and love so that we will not be hurt. Jesus warned against this in Matthew 24:12. He stated, "Because lawlessness is increased, most people's love will grow cold." If our love grows cold, then compassion is gone. There is no doubt that in our day lawlessness has increased. We must guard against our love growing cold as Jesus stated.

Read the verses below. After each one write a prayer to the Lord stating how this verse is or has been true in your life.

"You, O LORD, will not withhold Your compassion from me;
Your lovingkindness and Your truth will continually preserve me."
Psalm 40:11

____
____
____
____

"Be gracious to me, O God, according to Your lovingkindness;
According to the greatness of Your compassion blot out my transgressions."
Psalm 51:1

____
____
____
____

Now thank Him for being faithful to not only *feel* compassion toward you, but to be *moved by* compassion toward you.

Thank You, Father, for always being faithful to Your Word! Amen.

DAY 5: *Christ's Compassion*

Today I want us to examine the most precious display of Christ's compassion seen in Scripture. In only one book of the New Testament are we shown this very personal exchange between Jesus and two others whom He loved dearly. It only takes two verses to share in words what Jesus did, but it does not take much of an imagination to think about what was happening behind the words. Pray before you begin, asking the Lord to allow you to feel and somehow comprehend the compassion of Christ.

Before reading the chosen Scripture, let me share with you the setting and what is happening all around. During our lesson on forgiveness we studied what Jesus endured before going to the cross as well as what He endured while hanging on the cross. In our reading for today, Jesus is being crucified on the cross. The soldiers are dividing His garments among themselves. Then they decide, since the tunic was seamless, to cast lots for it to decide whose it shall be (see John 19:24). Now read John 19:25-27 and answer the questions that follow.

Who was standing by the cross (vs. 25)?

According to verse 26, who was also standing nearby?

Read John 21:20-24 to verify who this is. According to these verses, who do you think the disciple is?

Since we know that John wrote the book of John, we know that John is the "disciple whom Jesus loved." All throughout the book of John, this is how he describes himself. By describing himself in this manner, John is not inferring that he was loved more than the other disciples; this is how John saw himself—just as you and I should see ourselves. John knew that he was loved by Jesus. In fact, he knew it so well that this is the way that he describes himself four times in the book of John (see John13:23; 20:2; 21:7; 21:20).

Write what Jesus said to His mother (John 19:26). "_______________, _____________, _____________ _____________!"

Now write what Jesus said to John (vs. 27). "_______________, _______________ _______________!"

What a beautiful picture this is of Jesus Christ's love, mercy, and compassion toward His mother. Here He is struggling to breathe, so close to His very last breath, and He needs to take care of one last detail—His mother. Can you imagine the grief that overwhelmed her as she watched her son suffer and struggle so? Can you imagine how she must have wondered why this was happening? Can you imagine her thoughts and all the questions she had for God at that moment?

We have already studied Christ's willingness to have a one-on-one conversation with the thief who would soon join Him in paradise while others all around Him were sneering and mocking Him. Then in a moment, He looked down and saw His mother. What could He do? What could He say? Then He saw His disciple whom He dearly loved. He moved beyond feelings and moved into action. He entrusted them into one another's care. Not just that, but He took it a step further. He changed their relationship. He said to His mother, "This is now your son." And He said to John, "This is now your mother." He was not saying, "Take care of her for me." He was not saying, "Watch out for her for me." He was saying more: "Treat her as your own mother, for now she is!" and "Treat him as your own son, for now he is!" (my paraphrase). This is the ultimate in compassion. Jesus placed her needs before His own. He was suffering in pain and agony, and He still extended compassion. He wanted to make sure His mother had a son and his friend had a mother.

What does Scripture then state happened as a result of these two statements made by Jesus (vs. 27)?

Please do not miss the point that we have studied this week. Compassion is *caring enough to become involved in meeting someone's needs*.[16] A compassionate person channels those feelings into action. Jesus indeed did that over and over again, and especially here toward His mother. While dying He still felt mercy and then *expressed* compassion.

How does this display of compassion speak to you?

What does God want you to do differently because of this expression by Christ?

I have a dear friend who has a bad relationship with her mother. In many ways, her mother rejects her. Her mother is not pleased with anything that my friend does for her. If she buys her gifts, she returns them or tells them she doesn't need them. If she expresses love in actions, it is met with coldness. This has gone on for years. My friend has cried many tears over her mother's rejection. Yet, she continues to reach out to her and faithfully phones her every week, even in the face of coldness. The testimony to me has been how my dear friend continues to display love and compassion for her mother though she never receives affirmation of her mother's love in return. Once, as we were talking about the situation, she compared what she is to do for her mother to the story above. She said, "I feel like my relationship with my mother is to be like Jesus was to His mother. He loved her and cared for her, and that is what I am to do. However, I have given the care of her over to the Lord just as Jesus did to John. I say to the Lord, "Here is my mother; care for her. I am to continue to express love for her, but the Lord has the ultimate job of taking care of her because she won't allow me to."

Do you understand this type of display of love and compassion? My friend has Christ's heart toward her mother. She puts feelings into actions though they are not returned. She loves her mother unconditionally and has gained a heart of compassion toward her. She doesn't stop with saying loving things to her mother. She takes it further and still puts her love into action by calling her mother weekly, buying her mother gifts, taking care of her mother while she is ill, and the list goes on.

I would say that through abiding with Christ, my friend has been able to display the mind of Christ. Though her mother may not deserve compassion (we think), she gives it to her mother anyway. What about you?

Let's close with a little self-evaluation. Do you express compassion toward your:

Parents? Friends? Neighbors? Co-workers? Strangers in need?

Write below how the Lord has spoken to you this week. Then close by reading the verses listed about the compassion of God. ____

____

____

____

____

____

____

"The LORD is compassionate and gracious,
Slow to anger and abounding in lovingkindness."
Psalm 103:8

"He has made His wonders to be remembered;
The LORD is gracious and compassionate."
Psalm 111:4

"Light arises in the darkness for the upright;
He is gracious and compassionate and righteous."
Psalm 112:4

"Gracious is the LORD, and righteous;
Yes, our God is compassionate."
Psalm 116:5

Lord, teach us to have a heart like Jesus Christ and to be moved by compassion as He was. Amen.

Week 8

Jesus: His Example of Priorities and Rest

"And He said to them, 'Come away by yourselves to a secluded place and rest awhile.'" Mark 6:31

Day 1
Jesus Knew His Priorities

Day 2
Jesus Lived His Priorities

Day 3
The Result Is Rest

Day 4
Resting in Him

Day 5
The "REST" of the Story

Memory and Meditation Verse: "But seek first His kingdom and His righteousness, and all these things will be added to you." Matthew 6:33

Prayer: *Precious heavenly Father, I thank You and praise You for Your faithfulness to teach us so many things about You, Your Son, and ourselves. Thank You for loving us so much that You would patiently walk us through each lesson with Your guiding hand and gently teach us to walk as Jesus walked. Teach us this week about the importance of priorities and how to align ours according to Your will. Teach us about rest in this busy world we live in and what it truly means to rest in You. Teach us how to rely on You for our rest and to completely rest in Your promises. We welcome You, Lord, to do a mighty work in our lives once again this week.* ***Amen.***

Week 8

Jesus: His Example of Priorities and Rest

"And He said to them, 'Come away by yourselves to a secluded place and rest awhile.'" Mark 6:31

DAY 1: *Jesus Knew His Priorities*

This is another one of those lesson topics with concepts that completely intertwine. When I begin to talk about priorities, I can't get too far into the subject without talking about rest. When I talk about rest, I can't go far before priorities will begin to fall into the conversation. If you have your priorities in order, then you will rest more easily. If you feel the freedom to rest in a timely manner, and do so easily, then you most likely know your priorities. This is very important in today's society. We are made to believe that we must remain busy all the time! Busy can be good, but busy can be bad as well. It truly depends on what we are busy doing!

Today we want to look at Christ's example of His priorities and make sure we know what they are, so that we can examine our own priorities in light of God's Word. I have never experienced such freedom as I have when I learned what my priorities should be according to God's Word. Knowing these priorities makes a difference every day in every decision that I make. Jesus knew His priorities. He had no problem knowing what order His priorities were, unlike you and I. I probably should start by rephrasing the previous statement: Jesus knew His *priority*. It wasn't priorities, it was priority! Today we will look at what His priority was.

We will start by reading in Luke 4. Read verses 40-44 and answer the questions that follow. (Just so you don't get confused, this is the same situation we read about in our very first week on prayer. We studied Mark 1:28-37, but did not go past the part of the people finding Jesus praying).

As we studied before, Jesus spent an entire day and evening preaching, teaching, healing the sick, and casting out demons. In the early morning hours, where did Jesus go?

The crowds searched for Him, came to Him, and tried to do what?

Write down Jesus' complete response to them.

Based upon His response to the crowd, do you think Jesus knew what His priority was?

Now go back to Luke 4 and read verses 16-21. Based upon these verses, what would you say are Jesus Christ's priorities? List them on the following page:

1.

2.

3.

4.

5.

Look back over what you wrote and take note of each requirement of Christ. How many of the five requirements stated was Jesus sent to do for or to others?

"Just as the Son of Man did not come to be served, but to serve, and to give His life a ransom for many." Matthew 20:28

If Jesus Christ Himself (King of kings, Lord of lords) was sent to and was willing to serve others, then how much more should I be willing to serve others?

Have you ever thought about and wondered how Christ could live such a sacrificial, humble, and other-oriented life? I have many times, and I keep coming to the same conclusion no matter how long I think about it. The answer lies within John 4:34:

"Jesus said to them, 'My food is to do the will of Him who sent Me and to accomplish His work.'"

This is our answer! Jesus Christ's whole purpose and intention was to do the will of His Father and our Lord. In fact, this was so much of Christ's intention and priority that He claimed it was His very food. It was His nourishment. What else did Jesus say was His food?

This word translated "accomplish" (or "finish" in NIV) means "to bring to an end, complete, perfect." Based upon this verse, we can confidently say that Jesus received great delight in doing His Father's will and completing that which God gave Him to do. This was His priority.

What about you? Can you say the same for your life? What is your "food"? what provides your "nourishment" in life? I know we would all like to be able to say (like Christ) that doing the Father's will and accomplishing His work is what brings satisfaction and joy to our lives. If you are like me, when you experience these times of following His will (rather than your own) and completing an assignment from Him, then you are elated. There is truly no other feeling like it! However, if we are completely honest with ourselves, something much different may spring forth in answer to this question. Do not pass over this question too lightly. Sit before the Lord for a few moments, and let Him tell you what it is that you live for. What is your priority in life?

If this is hard to answer, then think over the last week or two and see what you have spent your time doing, energy accomplishing, and most of your concentration on. This will probably be a good indicator of what your priority is if God doesn't show up much in this self-evaluation.

____

____

____

____

What does Jesus advise us to do about our priorities? Read what He said in Matthew 6:33:

"But seek first His kingdom and His righteousness,
and all these things will be added to you."

According to this verse, what are we to seek first? ______________ ____________ and ________________ ________________. Then what happens? __________________________ ____________________________

This verse has been a theme verse in my life for many, many years. I remember a time years ago when I was stressed out, burned out, and pooped out! Let's just put it this way: I saw a little booklet one day in a Christian bookstore with the title, *Everybody's Breaking Pieces Off of Me,* and I bought it immediately. No thinking or pondering; I picked it up, bought it, and ran home to read it! That is truly how I felt. I was a young mother who didn't know how to tell anyone no—regardless of what they asked of me. I had three young children at home with my husband out of town for a month. We had just moved back to our home state and into a new house, and we faced a financial disaster immediately after moving in. On top of all that, we couldn't confront a single soul (regarding financial issues) because we believed the lie that we were not "good Christians" if we made any waves—no matter what! The Lord used the Truth of Matthew 6:33 to invade my soul and wash away many doubts, fears, and insecurities. I began to realize that if I had my priorities in proper order, I could say no and *know* that it was okay because I was following God's Truth rather than my own assumptions or preconceived ideas. I began to use this verse daily as God taught me to follow His plans each day and to seek His will for my life rather than base my day on the needs of the moment. I realized how very important it was to make Him my priority no matter what I faced each day and to spend time with Him in prayer and Bible study consistently. Slowly I began to feel freedom. He was the priority once again in my life, and everything else began to fall into its proper place as well. Read it again.

"But seek first His kingdom and His righteousness,
and all these things will be added to you."
Matthew 6:33

This word translated "seek" means "to seek and continue to seek." It is not a one-time action; rather, it is a continual action. We must continually seek Him first!

Do you know what your priorities are?

Hopefully you can say that you do and that the Lord is your No. 1 priority. But what about your second priority, and what is to be the third? We will get to that tomorrow! For now let's focus on making this verse a part of our very being. Memorize it, meditate on it, sing it, recite it, and live it! Jesus sought His Father's kingdom first no matter what the situation was. Will you be willing to do the same?

If you realize that He has not been your priority lately or ever, please take a moment and write your prayer of repentance and commitment to Him now. ___________________________

____

____

____

May God bless your seeking heart!

DAY 2: *Jesus Lived His Priorities*

Once you know your priorities, the rest is a matter of obedience. Knowing our priorities will result in living our priorities if obedience is the path that we choose. Since we have spent a whole week on obedience (week 2), we will not focus on that today; however, we will focus on how Jesus lived out His priorities and what we can learn from His example.

Living life guided by God's priorities for us makes living life much easier. I am not saying that the choices will come naturally—because they won't. We live in a society which emphasizes self-indulgence, self-gratification, and self always first! Jesus lived the complete opposite. Jesus lived life always putting others first. He met other people's needs, loved others who were unlovable, extended compassion to those who were judged as outcasts, and died on the cross so you and I could live eternally with the Father in heaven someday. Jesus came to serve others. We are those "others," and we have "others" all around us every day!

And as we serve others and put their needs before our own, our heavenly Father blesses us and fills us up even more so that we can have more of Him (His love, compassion, gentleness, mercy, and more) to give others.

We live in a society which bombards us with the message that we should serve ourselves and only then will we be ready to take care of others. That sounds very practical, and to our selfish flesh, it sounds very reasonable. However, this message goes straight against God's Word. How many times do you see in God's Word that we need to care for ourselves before we can care for others? How many Scripture references can you think of that tell you to serve yourself and then you will be ready to serve others? God's Word is the complete opposite of the lie that this world we live in gives us. We will easily buy into this lie if we are not careful. How and why? We see it, hear it, watch it, and cannot get away from it no matter where we turn. It is in magazines, TV shows, movies, advertising campaigns, on the Internet, and, unfortunately, it can be found in some churches. It sounds so believable, and since it feeds the desires of our flesh, we can easily fall into this trap set by the enemy. Be careful! The truth is that by abiding with our heavenly Father, we will be filled up by Him so that we can serve the "others" He has called us to serve first. In yesterday's lesson, I stressed how important it is to seek Him to know this. And as we serve others and put their needs before our own, our heavenly Father blesses us and fills us up even more so that we can have more of Him (His love, compassion, gentleness, mercy, and more) to give others. He guides us through each day and equips us for every situation He has *called us to*. In fact, the more we surrender ourselves to Him, the more we are actually able to accomplish. We will talk more about this in a few moments. For now, please stop and pray for God to show you His Truth regarding this rampant lie that invades our life on a daily basis.

Today we will begin in Matthew 6:25-34. Read it in its entirety and then answer the following questions:

In this passage Jesus is speaking against worry and anxiety, yet I believe this is applicable to priorities as well. According to this passage of Scripture, what is Jesus telling us to not worry about (vs. 25)?

Who takes care of the birds of the air?

Who is worth more than the birds?

According to verse 27, can our worries add any time to our lives?

Who clothes the grass of the field?

Jesus then states that we should not worry about what we will eat, drink, or wear because our heavenly Father knows that we ______________ (vs. 32) all these things. Then Jesus instructs us to do what (vs. 33)? "Seek ___________ His kingdom and His righteousness, and all these things will be ____________ to you."

R. C. Sproul states that when "Jesus said, 'Seek first,' the word *first* does not describe an initial step in a numerical sequence. Rather, the force of the term is to emphasize *priority of importance*. Our top priority is to seek God's kingdom and God's righteousness."[17] You see, as we seek His kingdom and His righteousness, all the other pieces of our lives fall into place.

Have you ever realized that seeking His kingdom and His righteousness as a priority requires that all you strive for in life revolves around Him and *His* priorities for your life? How are you doing at seeking His priorities for your life?

Now go back to Matthew 6 and read verse 24. Based on this verse, would you say that you have tried or are trying to serve two masters?

If so, what is your struggle with? In other words, what do you put before God?

It could be one thing or person, or it could be many things or people. Priorities are hard to get into line without a lot of self-evaluation and wisdom from the Lord. Look at the following list and write a *1* beside your top priority, *2* by your next, and so on until you get to *5*.

Children	Career	Home	Extended Family
Ministry	God	Exercise	
Hobbies	Spouse	Friends	

Now write below what you believe your priorities should be:

1.
2.
3.
4.
5.

Each of our lists might look a little different. However, one thing is for sure: God is to be the No. 1 priority for each of us. Since I am married with children, my spouse should be second and my children third. This is one area where many women make a mistake. Mothers and fathers can easily put their children before their relationship with their spouse. This is not at all what God planned for us. Your spouse (for men and women) should be your No. 2 priority, which would make your spouse your No. 1 human relationship! Wow, what changes would be made in marriages across the world and in our churches if couples could grasp this truth! Yes, I am saying that your marriage partner should be your No. 2 priority if you are a man *or* woman. Your marriage partner should come before your children, your career, everything except your relationship with the Lord. Then your children should be your third priority, but only after your spouse and never before!

We cannot confuse our ministry work with our time alone with the Lord.

What happens next in our list of priorities? Sometimes it can become a little more difficult at this point. For me, my home falls into the fourth-place position right after my children. Titus 2:3-5 and Proverbs 31:10-31 make this very clear. The Lord never meant for me to place church work, career, or ministry work above our family or before my home. (I am mainly talking to women now.) The wonderful truth is that my husband, children, and my home *are my ministry*. Titus 2:3-5 details what older women should be and do as well as what they should teach the younger women to be and do. Proverbs 31:10-31 is known as a scriptural example of what a godly (or excellent) wife looks like. Considering the three verses in Titus and the twenty-one verses in Proverbs, one can see how much of a woman's focus is to be on marriage, her children, and her home. I believe God desires for a woman to have a heart for her home and those in her home. Can I do or have more? Absolutely! What about a job outside the home—is this possible? Of course it is, but not if I can't keep my priorities in order. I believe the Proverbs 31 woman contributed financially to her household, but I also believe she was still able to keep her priorities in their proper order. (These passages are studied in detail in my Bible study *Called to Be a Keeper.)* The same would go for men. They can't sacrifice the needs and responsibilities of their family for the sake of career ambitions.

An important point needs to be made here. Please listen closely. We cannot confuse our ministry work with our time alone with the Lord. Please think about this before moving on. *We cannot confuse ministry for our time alone with the Lord.* The two are separate priorities. At this point in my life, God has called me to teach God's Word and write this Bible study. I gave up a career once to stay at home with my children because I could not do both, nor did I want to. Later in life I gave up a thriving home-based business to teach women's Bible studies because that is what God called me to do. I did not want to give up the business because I thoroughly enjoyed it and believed in it. However, I wanted to seek His kingdom first and I (personally) could not do both and keep the top four priorities in their proper order. Right now as I complete this Bible study, I look back upon this busy season in my life. It has been hard, and my family has had to make sacrifices. However, we talked about what the requirement would be for all of us before I committed to do this. They and I realized it is a busy season of life and only a short time. They have "picked up the slack" and supported me all the way by doing extra chores, doing more around the house, and giving up time with me due to deadlines. Yes, there will always be seasons in our lives when things get busy. Deal with these times together, and make sure it does not become a *way of life*. No matter how busy we become, we should never push God out of first place, and never should allow our husbands, children, or homes to suffer during these busy times.

Now let's get back to Jesus and His example to us regarding priorities. As we studied in the previous weeks, Jesus knew what He was sent to do because He abided with the Father and sought His Father. What about you? How will you know what you are sent here to do? Once again, we follow the example of Jesus. We abide with the Father so that we will bear fruit and the Father will be glorified (see John 15:8). As we abide with Him, we will seek Him just as stated in Matthew 6:33. His priorities will become our priorities!

Let's take a look into a powerful statement made by Christ recorded in the book of John. Read John 8:28-29 below and answer the questions that follow.

"So Jesus said, 'When you lift up the Son of Man, then you will know that I am* He, *and I do nothing on My own initiative, but I speak these things as the Father taught Me. And He who sent Me is with Me; He has not left Me alone, for I always do the things that are pleasing to Him.'"

According to these verses, does Jesus do anything on His own initiative?

What things does Jesus speak?

Finally, what things does Jesus do?

The Greek word translated "pleasing" means "to be pleasing, agreeable."

And how often does Jesus do these things?
Circle one: sometimes never always

Yes, Jesus Himself said that He always does the things that are pleasing to the Father.

If Jesus always sought to please the Father, how much more should I?

Jesus knew His priorities, and He knew His ultimate priority was to please the Father. What is your ultimate priority in life? Is it truly to please Him? If it is, then you will spend time making sure that you have your other priorities in order so that you can live that abundant fruit-filled life that He has planned for you. Before you put this away today, spend some time in prayer asking Him how you may need to adjust your priorities so that you live a life in which you *always* do things that are pleasing to Him! Write your answers from Him below.

Father, show us how we need to readjust our lives so that we will always please You and be a reflection of Your Son. Amen.

DAY 3: *The Result Is Rest*

Thankfully we have learned what was and is a priority to Christ. It isn't that we didn't know this before; it was a matter of focusing in on it and seeing for ourselves what God's Word has to say. We now know "Who" is to be a priority to us as well. Since we know what our priorities are to be, we must practice putting them into place. For some of us, this will come more naturally than for others. Some of us have a hard time letting go of things that we want to do, but feel we no longer should do. For others of us, this realization of priorities becomes very freeing as we begin to give up things that are no longer necessary because we see they are not a requirement from the Lord.

When your aim is to live a life pleasing to the Lord, then it becomes easier to say no to others and to other responsibilities that you know are not required of you. Why? Because rather than trying to please to men, you care more about pleasing the Lord. If you find it difficult to say no to others who make requests of you and of your time (even good things), then keep Galatians 1:10 at the forefront of your thoughts. Memorize it, carry it, and repeat it over and over every time you worry about saying no to someone because of what they may think of you. Keep seeking Him as well, and your ability to say no will become easier as your priorities become crystal clear!

Today we want to look at Christ's example regarding rest. Read Mark 6:7-13 to understand the setting of the story. Then turn to Luke 9 and read verses 1-6 to get another perspective before answering the questions below.

Jesus had summoned the twelve for a specific purpose. Jesus gave them specific instructions about what to take with them, what to wear, how to enter a town, and how to leave a town. According to Luke 9:1, what power and authority had Jesus given them?

Based on verse 2, what else had He sent them out to do?

Now turn back to Mark 6. According to verses 12 and 13, what did the twelve do?

Based upon all that you just read, did the twelve do what Jesus had called and instructed them to do? Do you think this was hard work?

I cannot imagine the drain this was to the twelve men God had called. I know that God equipped them to do the job, but do not think for a moment that it was easy. I know that my pastor speaks of how tired he is after the Sunday sermon that he shares twice in a morning. I never understood this until God began calling me to teach women's Bible studies and speak to various groups. The preparation that goes into it can be exhausting. But, even more exhausting than the preparation is what happens after it is over. The mental, spiritual, and emotional drain that I feel after I have been given a message by the Lord and then delivered it is incredible. It is exhilarating no doubt, but exhausting as well!

So, here the twelve men chosen by Christ were given power and authority to cast out demons and to heal diseases and to proclaim the kingdom of God. They have just gone out and done exactly what Jesus had instructed them to do. Now let's find out what happens when they return to Jesus. Read Mark 6:30-32 and answer the questions below.

What did the apostles report to Jesus?

What was Christ's response to them? (vs. 31) "Come away by yourselves to a secluded place and ______________ a while."

In verse 32 we are told that they went away by themselves to a secluded place. After reading this you might think that the apostles went by themselves to a particular secluded place; however, turn to Luke 9:10 to see who led them there.

Who led them to this secluded place (Bethsaida)?

Again, what was the purpose for going there? To r_________!

Jesus was teaching the apostles and us how important it is to rest. The Greek word translated "rest" in this verse is *anapauo* and it means "to give intermission from labor, to give rest, to refresh."[18] The way the Lord used this to speak to me is not only how important it is to rest and to have an intermission from labor, but also that *Jesus took* them for this time of refreshing. Who are we to go to for refreshing?

Read the verses below that describe God.

"Your lovingkindness, O LORD, extends to the heavens,
Your faithfulness reaches to the skies.
Your righteousness is like the mountains of God;
Your judgments are like a great deep.
O LORD, You preserve man and beast.
How precious is Your lovingkindness, O God!
And the children of men take refuge in the shadow of Your wings.
They drink their fill of the abundance of Your house;
And You give them to drink of the river of Your delights.
For with You is the fountain of life;
In Your light we see light."
Psalm 36:5-9

Isn't this exciting? Read again the last two lines of these verses. When we are worn out, tired, exhausted, drained, and strained, we are to go to the only One who can truly satisfy. When we need refreshment, when we are dry, when we are "worn slick," when we are parched and thirsty—where do we turn? We turn to God who is the fountain of life. He is the source of life. We turn to God to meet our need for refreshment. It is God Himself who will fill us to overflowing when we turn to Him for our rest and our refreshment.

We certainly have seen throughout our study how Jesus went to God for everything. How precious to us that here in these few verses we see Jesus take the apostles aside for some much needed rest. *The only one who can truly provide rest to us led the apostles away to receive rest from Him.* I believe the Lord Jesus gave them more than just a cessation from labor. I believe that just as He provides for you and me when we seek our rest from Him, He also willingly gave them refreshment and rest *in* Him.

We live in a world that perpetuates busyness. For some of us that is a challenge. For some of us it is not. Some of us fight against laziness. I have been there! Some of us fight against slowing down. I have been there too! We need to live a balanced life. Our world is on the "fast track." It is to the point for many of us that if we don't have ourselves or our children in a million activities (even church activities), then we feel as though we have failed or are failing at something. I would dare to say that if you cannot enjoy some quiet time, peaceful times, every now and then, then you might need to learn to rest. A person who can rest (when appropriate) is usually a person who has the character trait of contentment. My husband and I work hard on this issue with two of our children. We have one who never wants to stop or slow down. This particular child is most happy when something is happening! Before one activity is finished or at the brink of ending, this one is already looking forward to "what's next?" Then we have another child who in many ways is the complete opposite. This particular child could live as a couch potato and be happy "vegging out" all day, almost every day! Are both children wrong? No and yes. No, if these attitudes remain in moderation, and yes, if each child lived this way to the extreme. We all need balance in our lives.

A balanced, godly person is one who knows their priorities in life. This person seeks to please the Father and does nothing on their own initiative. This person also knows that they need rest and that rest comes from the Lord. They do God's kingdom work and then turn to Him for that refreshment. *This person knows, like Christ, that there is a time to do God's work and a time to rest physically.* Proper priorities equal proper rest. Balanced people get filled back up so they can go back to do more kingdom work. They are busy serving others, but not at the expense of their families. They know very well the difference between their time alone with the Lord and their ministry work for the Lord. This person understands their purpose on this earth and clearly strives to achieve that very goal. In fact, this godly, balanced person usually can "run circles" around others. I have personally watched people who get more done and accomplish more for the Lord than someone who is striving in their own power to meet needs and get the to-do list complete. I have often wondered how these people get more done than others, and I seem to come to the same conclusion each time: When one is seeking the Lord for what to do while making Him the priority, then all that God wants done gets done! How? As we follow His will and do things His way. Then these same people are always brimming over with God's peace and joy. It doesn't mean they are so busy that they never stop, because they do. In fact, these people are probably more rested than others who are "striving in their own way" to get His work done. You see, when we have all our priorities in order, we are comfortable to rest. We are comfortable to rest because we know that God's intention is for us to rest. His will is for us to rest from His work, but to turn to Him for that rest as well. This is what we will cover tomorrow.

How has God spoken to you today? Record any thoughts or changes that you need to make. ____
____
____
____

Thank You, dear Lord, for knowing our need for rest even when we don't! Amen.

DAY 4: *Resting in Him*

Not long ago while our family was on vacation, we stopped briefly at a convenience store. While I was waiting, I picked up a magazine that is owned and operated by a very well-known talk show host. As I read the short introduction to this particular issue, I was humored by her logic regarding rest. She was writing about how she had experienced burn out many times in her career. She was sharing her answer to this problem and what a difference it has made in her life. She labeled it as being "recharged or refueled" each week. She then went on to explain how she uses one day each week to refill, recharge, or refuel. (I can't remember the exact terminology.) She uses this entire day for herself to do what she wants to do, even if it is nothing at all. She says that she needs this to maintain the pace of her life and to be a better person. She says that the day of the week that she chose was Sunday, because Sunday works best for her. What struck me as amusing is that she shared this as if it were her idea. I sarcastically (just a bit) thought, "What a novel idea, though not yours at all. God laid out this type of plan for His children when He created them and gave them guidelines to live by." You see, God meant for us to rest (to have intermission from labor, to refresh). He knew that we needed rest to continue doing His work.

Read the verses below, and then answer the questions.

"Come to Me, all who are weary and heavy-laden, and I will give you rest. Take My yoke upon you and learn from Me, for I am gentle and humble in heart, and you will find rest for your souls. For My yoke is easy and My burden is light." Matthew 11:28-30

Who does Jesus tell to come to Him?

What will He give to those who are weary and heavy-laden?

Jesus then said to take His yoke upon you and to _______________ from Him.

What does Jesus then say that He is? __________________ and ______________ in heart. Then He tells us that if we do this, we will what? Find ______________ for our souls. According to Christ, His yoke is ________________ and His burden is ______________.

When you are weary and burdened, do you go to Jesus? Do you seek rest from Christ when you are in distressing and difficult circumstances?

Jesus wants us to seek Him for rest. He wants us to understand that it is He who gives us the rest we need to live the abundant life that He has for us. We can't get this type of rest from vitamins, healthy dieting, strenuous workouts, or anything else. Though all these things are good for us and our body, this is not what Jesus meant for us. Yes, God meant for us to rest physically. He meant for us to have a time to be refreshed. But did you know that He also wants to provide "rest for our souls"?

Jesus tells us in verse 28 that He will give us rest. This word translated "rest" is the same as we studied yesterday (intermission from labor, to give rest, to refresh). However, in verse 29 where Jesus states, "You will find rest for your souls," the word has a slightly different meaning. I find it interesting that this word translated "rest" is the same Greek word as used for the previous rest, except it is used as a noun instead of a verb. Read the following regarding this word for rest:

> Christ's "rest" is not a "rest" from work, but in work, "not the rest of inactivity but of the harmonious working of all the faculties and affections—of will, heart, imagination, conscience—because each has found in God the ideal sphere for its satisfaction and development."[19]

You see, we can find rest physically and be refreshed with Christ in our rest. But I believe that (as always) Jesus wants to give us so much more than that. Jesus wants us to rest inwardly through Him. He wants to provide rest for our souls. There is not another place or thing that can provide this type of rest. Spiros Zodhiates defines it this way: "the inward tranquility while one performs necessary labor. In Matt 11:29, the Lord promises *anapausis* (inner tranquility)."[20] What a precious gift this is from the Lord. He waits to give us this inner tranquility. Jesus is waiting to give you rest for your soul. He wants to give you His peace and His contentment. The only thing that will keep you from receiving it is you.

"Ask, and it will be given to you; seek, and you will find; knock, and it will be opened to you. For everyone who asks receives, and he who seeks finds, and to him who knocks it will be opened." Matthew 7:7-8

It may be harder for us to rest inwardly than physically, but Jesus wants us to do both. Do you seek inward tranquility from Him? Asked another way, do you seek rest from Him? If you answered no, then write down whatever it is that consumes your thoughts right now, worries you, and distracts you. ____

____

____

____

____

Now give the list to Him in prayer. Tell Him that you want to find rest for your soul in Him and then do it by naming each item listed and laying them at His feet and leaving them at His throne. Jesus has told you that He desires for you to come to Him and "find rest for your soul." Go to Him now. He truly is the only one who can give you this rest. *His rest is a sustaining rest; it is not a fleeting rest.*

Jesus tells us in His Word that the harvest is plentiful and the workers are few (see Matthew 9:37). As Christians, we can easily become overwhelmed by what needs to be done, but we won't if we seek Him first, do nothing on our own initiative, and strive to please Him above all else. In fact, it will be Him who we hear telling us, "Come away to a secluded place with Me and rest, for it is I who will provide rest for your soul."

God bless you as you seek to rest in Him!

DAY 5: *The "REST" of the Story*

Here we are together at the last day of the last lesson. My heart has hungered for this moment, and at the same time I have dreaded this moment's arrival. I have come to this point with very mixed emotions. There is a part of me that is ecstatic to be able to complete this assignment that the Lord has given to me. To be able to see it come to a close because of the weekly deadlines and the pressure that it has placed on my family and on me gives me a sense of relief. However, there is a much larger part of me that will miss watching God move in me, work with me to get me to understand what His will is and what He wanted to teach me, and translate that into words on paper. I know as I continue to study His Word I will see Him, His hand, and His touch in the same ways and in many new ways. However, at this particular point in my life, I have faced this new territory with Him in a very intimate and personal way. I will never forget this time and will be eternally grateful to have shared it with Him and with you. Thank you for joining me in this journey. Now is the time to bring it to a close!

Today I would like for us to go back to a few verses that we have already looked at this week. Please read the verses from John below.

"So Jesus said, 'When you lift up the Son of Man, then you will know that I am He, and I do nothing on My own initiative, but I speak these things as the Father taught Me. And He who sent Me is with Me; He has not left Me alone, for I always do the things that are pleasing to Him.'" John 8:28-29

We have looked at these verses intently this week, but I would like to share with you one more truth that the Holy Spirit revealed to me during my time studying these verses. We have made it clear that Jesus does nothing on His own initiative; He only speaks what He has been taught and He always does the things that are pleasing to His Father. Based on these two verses, who does Jesus say *taught* Him?

Now look at the verses we studied yesterday.

"Come to Me, all who are weary and heavy-laden, and I will give you rest. Take My yoke upon you and learn from Me, for I am gentle and humble in heart, and you will find rest for your souls." Matthew 11:28-29

Jesus tells us to come to Him for rest. He tells us to take His yoke upon ourselves and that He is gentle and humble in heart. He also tells us that by doing this we will find rest for our souls. Complete this statement made by Jesus in verse 29: "Take My yoke upon you and ________________ from Me." Who are we to learn from?

Based on the previous questions pertaining to John 8:28-29, who teaches Jesus?

This is what Jesus was sent by the Father to do and to be for us. We needed a Savior. God provided that Savior by sending Jesus to die on the cross for our sins. But as always, God has multiple purposes in all that He does. God sent Jesus, whom He (our heavenly Father) taught to be an example to us so that we could learn from Him (Jesus) how to live. God left Jesus Christ's perfect example on how to live written all over the pages of Scripture so that we could learn from Jesus and Him. Jesus was *taught* by the Father (see John 8:28), and we are to *learn* from Jesus (see Matthew 11:29).

The Greek word translated "learn" in Matthew 11:29 is *manthano*. It means "to learn by inquiry, or observation, of learning Christ, not simply the doctrine of Christ, but Christ Himself, a process not merely of getting to know the person but of so applying the knowledge as to walk differently from the rest of the Gentiles."[21]

That is what my desire has always been for myself and for those who would do this study. It is that we would live our lives in such a way that we would walk differently from the rest of the world. We should live as Christ lived, and we should handle situations as Christ would. We should seek in God's Word the example of Jesus so that we would know how to pray, obey, deal with temptation, love, forgive, confront others, extend compassion, prioritize our lives, rest physically, and rest in Him so that others everywhere would be drawn to Him through us. We need to be Jesus Christ's shadow, His reflection. We should follow Him so intently that when people see us, they see Him. My desire and prayer is that they see you and I following His example so closely that we are but a mere shadow of the cross, thereby giving glory and honor to our Father.

Read the following verses prayerfully. Write your *prayer of desire* to the Lord after each one. Use these as a constant reminder and an encouragement to you.

"The one who says he abides in Him ought himself to walk in the same manner as He walked."
1 John 2:6

Will you walk in the same manner as Jesus? ____________________________________

____

____

____

♦

"Have this attitude in yourselves which was also in Christ Jesus."
Philippians 2:5

Will you keep the attitude of Jesus? ____

____

____

____

♦

"For you have been called for this purpose, since Christ also suffered for you, leaving you an example for you to follow in His steps."
1 Peter 2:21

Following Christ requires suffering. Are you willing to suffer for Jesus? ______________
____
____
____

♦

"For I gave you an example that you also should do as I did to you."
John 13:15

Will you live a life following the example of Christ? ______________________________
____
____
____

How does one "wrap something up" that should never end? I believe this is only the beginning of studying Jesus, Our Perfect Example. He is and will always remain our perfect example, the One we turn to and seek when we need to know how we are to live.

"And there are also many other things which Jesus did, which if they were written in detail, I suppose that even the world itself would not contain the books that would be written."

John 21:25

May God richly bless your time in His Word!

In His Love,
Lori Merrill

Jesus, Our Perfect Example

The Father sent His Son to teach us,
He taught us as the Father did the Son,
He taught us to live a life that is pleasing,
So that many souls would be won.

To always turn to the Father in prayer
Is the way that Jesus lived,
To walk in obedience humbly,
Even to death He still would give.

To know how to face this life of temptation,
Yet to live successfully still,
While loving others undeserving,
To make this choice against my will.

To look past their sins to their need,
Jesus forgave like this again and again.
Even while confronting another,
His purpose was restoration—a turning from the sin.

To be moved by the needs of others,
This is the compassion that Jesus felt,
Seek Him first and His kingdom,
So that at His throne my soul is knelt.

Yes, Jesus walked this path before me,
He walked it so that I could plainly see
What the truth of those few words mean,
"Deny yourself and follow Me."

His example I am to follow,
And like Jesus may my example be,
A mere shadow of the cross to others,
The reflection of Him coming from me.

Lori Merrill
April 2, 2003

Endnotes

[1] *Enhanced Strong's Lexicon* (Oak Harbor, WA: Logos Research Systems, Inc., 1995).

[2] *Enhanced Strong's Lexicon*.

[3] Robert L. Thomas, ThD, ed., *New American Standard Hebrew-Aramaic and Greek Dictionaries, Updated Edition* (Anaheim, CA: Foundation Publications, Inc., 1999, c1998).

[4] *Enhanced Strong's Lexicon*.

[5] *The New American Standard Bible, 1995 Update* (La Habra, CA: The Lockman Foundation, 1996).

[6] *Enhanced Strong's Lexicon*.

[7] *Enhanced Strong's Lexicon*.

[8] Donald Whitney, *Spiritual Disciplines for the Christian Life* (Colorado Springs, CO: NavPress, 1991), 17.

[9] W. E. Vine, *Vine's Expository Dictionary of Biblical Words* (Nashville, TN: Thomas Nelson, 1985).

[10] J. Vernon McGee, Thru the Bible with J. Vernon McGee (Nashville, TN: Thomas Nelson Publishers, 1983), 353.

[11] Webster's New World Dictionary, Third College Edition, s.v. "confront."

[12] Bruce H. Wilkinson, Executive Editor, *Family Walk Again* (Grand Rapids: Zondervan Publishing House, 1993), 201.

[13] John F. Walvoord and Roy B. Zuck, *The Bible Knowledge Commentary* (Wheaton, IL: Scripture Press Publications, Inc., 1983, 1985).

[14] *Family Walk Again* (Grand Rapids: Zondervan Publishing House, 1993), 201.

[15] Stuart K. Webber, *Holman New Testament Commentary on Matthew* (Broadman & Holman through Logos, 2000).

[16] *Family Walk Again,* 201.

[17] R. C. Sproul, "Righteousness Exalts a Nation," *Focus on the Family*, April/May 2003.

[18] *Vine's Expository Dictionary of Biblical Words*.

[19] *Vine's Expository Dictionary of Biblical Words*.

[20] Spiros Zodhiates, *The Complete Word Study Dictionary: New Testament (electronic edition),* (Chattanooga, TN: AMG Publishers).

[21] *Vine's Expository Dictionary of Biblical Words*.